ABOUT THE AUTHOR

STEVE DOOCY is an Emmy Award–winning broadcaster and the cohost of *Fox & Friends* on the Fox News Channel. He has earned reporting and writing awards from the Associated Press, Sigma Delta Chi, and the National Academy of Television Arts and Sciences, and has worked at NBC, CBS, and Fox. He and his wife, Kathy, live just outside New York City with their three children, who grow up over the course of these two hundred some-odd pages.

TALES
FROM
THE
Dad SIDE

Also by Steve Doocy

The Mr. & Mrs. Happy Handbook

TALES
FROM
THE
DAD SIDE

Mis adventures in Fatherhood

STEVE DOOCY

HARPER

NEW YORK • LONDON • TORONTO • SYDNEY

HARPER

A hardcover edition of this book was published in 2008 by William Morrow, an imprint of HarperCollins Publishers.

HarperCollins books may be purchased for educational, business, or sales promotional use. For information please write: Special Markets Department, HarperCollins Publishers, 10 East 53rd Street, New York, NY 10022.

FIRST HARPER PAPERBACK PUBLISHED 2009.

Designed by Chris Welch

The Library of Congress has catalogued the hardcover edition as follows:
Doocy, Steve.
    Tales from the dad side : misadventures in fatherhood / Steve Doocy.—1st ed.
        p. cm.
    ISBN 978-0-06-144162-2
1. Fatherhood.   2. Fatherhood—Humor.   I. Title.
    HQ756.D577 2008
    306.874'20973—dc22   2008025914

ISBN 978-0-06-144163-9 (pbk.)

09 10 11 12 13   DIX/RRD   10 9 8 7 6 5 4 3 2 1

To my father, of course

There are three stages of a man's life: he believes in Santa Claus, he doesn't believe in Santa Claus, he is Santa Claus.

—Author not known
(but obviously a dad)

CONTENTS

FOREWORD

Why, you're asking yourself, does this guy think he's an expert on the topic of fatherhood? Forget the fact that I hosted a network show on parenting—I only did that for the catering. The fact is that as a longtime professional journalist I have been observing my father for fifty years, not counting the twenty years I've chronicled my own children, for a sum total of seventy years, which is remarkable for a fifty-year-old guy. This is the same math logic I use to calculate my taxes.

"You want to be a dad on a sitcom?"

That was what the legendary chairman of NBC, Brandon Tartikoff, asked me, wondering if I wanted to be a wisecracking albeit misguided father on a situation comedy for one half hour each week. I'd be the peacock network's latest version of Bill Cosby, who at that same time was making hundreds of millions of dollars as he dispensed heartfelt advice that always ended with a punch line to his camera-perfect children, who were not really his children but highly compensated actors pretending to be blood relatives.

"Steve, you *look* like the perfect dad," the NBC chairman added after I taped my show at 30 Rock.

I look like the perfect dad? That seemed odd because at that moment I was wearing heavy Pan-Cake makeup and a bib. To the best of my knowledge, the perfect dad does not wear eyeliner and a bib, unless it's cross-dresser night at Red Lobster.

Instead I returned to television news and I did not take that sit-com job, which ran almost a decade and made the guy who did take the job tens of millions of dollars. My wife just showed me a photo layout of him in a recent *In Style* magazine surrounded by supermodels on his private island lighting a cigar with a fifty.

There's more to fatherhood than looking the part; a real dad is someone who would do *anything* for his kids. My friend Mary, whose father was a legendary columnist during Hollywood's golden era, didn't know how to break some bad news to her dad. A clever, proud man, he was in his eighties and had slowed down a bit—he made Larry King look like Billy Elliot.

"Dad, I've got MS."

Stunned, the father said nothing for a moment. Mary could see the wheels in his head turning. "Don't you worry, we are going to lick this thing," he said. "Do you want me to call Jerry Lewis's people?"

Mary paused to reflect on his generous offer of cashing in one of show business's most valuable assets, a favor.

"Look, Jerry owes me big. So does Dean, but I can't collect from him, he and Sammy are long gone," the former scribbler for *Variety, Hollywood Reporter,* and *TV Guide* confided to his girl.

"Dad, calling Jerry Lewis's people would be great if I had *muscular dystrophy*," Mary replied, "but I have *multiple sclerosis*. Maybe you could call Annette Funicello's people?"

Disease confusion.

Fathers are generally *big-picture guys* who get all sorts of important details scrambled: diseases that start with the letter *m*, birthdays, times of school events, and with painful frequency even the names of their own children. Generally mothers never make those kinds of mistakes, because while they're both parents, dads are different from moms.

That could be the greatest understatement since Noah turned on the Weather Channel and found out that the next forty days called for a 20 percent chance of light rain.

Mothers are reassuring comforters and healers who dole out unconditional love, while fathers are the family muscle, the providers, the tire-gauge-in-the-pocket practical guys who twice yearly try to be romantic.

"Roses, on a Tuesday?" Mom observed as Dad walked through the door. "Were you stopped at the light again?"

While there is no disputing that nine months of pregnancy is rough on a woman, she should walk a mile in a father's Hush Puppies with thirty or forty pounds of wiggling kid around her neck for the first five years of a child's life. Seeing a father able to stand up straight after a full day of piggyback rides without a trip to the chiropractor would be as remarkable as seeing Mary-Kate Olsen finish an entire niçoise salad.

"Pops, what time's curfew?" Cain asked his father, Adam.

"Be home before *CSI Mesopotamia.*"

"But Dad . . ."

"All right, ask your mother."

That was not what the youngster wanted to hear, because everybody knew his mother, Eve, wore the fig leaf in that family.

History has shown us that ever since the beginning, moms and dads have been different. In reality, new moms are better at parenting than new dads, but there's a reason why: they are programmed to mother. What is playing with a doll if not mommy practice? In fact, there is a mega mother industrial complex made up of thousands of magazines, books, classes, and TV shows that instruct women on how to raise the perfect child. Once a week Oprah tells how to do it despite never having raised a child, unless you count Dr. Phil.

Spontaneously upon umbilical cord snipping they become lifelong members of a special sorority with every other mom, which explains how my wife was speaking to a total stranger on a buffet line when the woman confessed, "Forget knee pain, honey, I had an episiotomy with sixty-nine stitches." Vaguely familiar with the procedure, I quietly crossed my legs and politely nodded in horror.

So they have a vast mommy-wing conspiracy. Meanwhile, across the gender aisle, fathers are usually clueless about what to do with that new baby at home. I considered it a good father-son outing if I didn't accidentally break off an arm even though he had a spare. This is what happens to an entire species that has no special father TV shows, zero *Maxim* articles on "Nine Simple Cures for Diaper Rash," and certainly no practice-dad toys. If you think G.I. Joe inculcates in a boy how to be a father, you're nuts. G.I. Joe is not something to cuddle. He's not even a toy. G.I. Joe is a molded plastic killing machine, and let's keep it that way.

In grade school my brothers-in-law were momentarily fascinated by their sister's Betsy Wetsy, to the point that they disemboweled her to see the doll magic that made her piddle. After their fact-finding jackknife surgery they returned the doll to the crib, where she was still fed her bottle, despite the fact that from that day forward Betsy peed from her armpit.

So a man doesn't have much of a foundation in fathering. It's more on-the-job training, and it starts the day he becomes a father, which for me was the greatest day ever. Those stories about how life changes are absolutely true. On the birthday of my first child, when I walked out of that hospital, the sky seemed bluer, food tasted better, and the songs on the radio were happy and apparently written just for me! I had a reason to be on earth; I was somebody's dad.

I would witness my kid's first steps, first haircuts, and the bloody loss of his first teeth. I am, however, not Superman. Nobody can be there for everything, which is how I can live with myself for being on the mower when my son said his first words, which my wife insists were "trust fund."

Note to self: No more motivational baby books by Donald Trump.

As I prepared this book for publication I asked my daughter Mary, who'd known only a childhood in the leafy suburbs of New York, if she had any idea what my childhood was like growing up on the flatlands of America's Great Plains.

"Not really," she started, but "I bet you sat around and popped a bunch of corn pills."

For the record, I did not spend my Wonder Years lurking outside a Kansas grain elevator in some sort of a corn silk coma. But she proved what I had believed to be true—she didn't know much about my life, which was not the case when I asked her about her mother's history.

"Mommy had a convertible with a personalized plate that was BLUIZ, and that gray-haired guy on CBS took her to a Halloween dance." She continued with such detail about her mother's personal narrative that if there had been a piano sound track, it would have sounded like an episode of A&E's *Biography*.

Mary didn't know much about my life before she came along be-cause just like my father and his peers in the Greatest Generation, we don't like to talk much about ourselves. Some don't want to brag; others don't want to bore. Personally, after a hard day at work I'd rather go home and listen to their daily dramas from school rather than gossip over the dinner table about which of my associates was stealing office supplies.

These stories are all true, which will prompt some of you to ques-tion why I have not yet been charged with endangering a child or impersonating a parent.

While I have a highly visible job on the *Fox & Friends* program, in real life my wife and family are the stars. Kathy, my wife of more than twenty years, really deserves the *complete credit* for the wonderful children who were raised at our house. Allow me to introduce them: they are Peter, Mary, and Sally, whose names we have abbreviated for necklace-engraving purposes to *PMS*.

The other person who casts a long shadow over this work is my own father, Jim Doocy, who in 2008 finally retired after sixty-two years of working for the man. Now he has more free time to chat with me on the phone, which is terrific for me because he always has a great idea about how I can fix a carburetor, shingle the garage, or vacuum the refrigerator coil. He's good with mechanical things; however, some of the newfangled digital stuff dumbfounds him. "Stephen, check your fax machine," he told me this morning. "I sent you a fax. After you read it, send it back—it's my only copy."

I could tell him that the original is still in *his* machine, but there's no reason for me to lecture him. Like many, he thinks the facsimile machine is like the transporter from *Star Trek*, magically transmitting whole sheets of paper through the phone lines. But I won't tell him how it really works, because I don't want to hurt his feelings. He's the only dad I'll ever have, which means I am honest and direct with him much the same way the Macaroni Grill is an Italian restaurant—not so much.

TALES

FROM

THE

Dad SIDE

1

Birth

Dad on Arrival

July 21, 1987, was the day I became a father. My wife, Kathy, had gotten pregnant nine months earlier on or around my thirtieth birthday party with things we had around the house.

My wife had been having contractions for over a month, and the doctor decided to induce the labor during the hottest, most humid stretch of the year, on the kind of day when Angelina Jolie would try to adopt a kid from Antarctica. For my wife's induced delivery we showed up very early at the east door of the George Washington University Hospital, just a few blocks from the White House. This was the same trauma center where six years earlier they rushed President Reagan, when the world discovered that John Hinckley liked Jodie Foster in a much stranger way than Joanie ever loved Chachi.

We have a very romantic story. I met my wife for the first time when she was five. We weren't neighbors or schoolmates or even vague acquaintances. I saw her on television, where she starred as the most incredible girl in the world, Mattel's talking doll, Chatty Cathy. Pull a string in her neck and without moving her lips she'd start repeating one of numerous recorded sentences, bossing around whoever was unlucky enough to be holding her.

"Please change my dress."

"May I have some tea, Mummy?"

"Will you play with me?"

A limited conversationalist, she'd incessantly repeat the same handful of demands over and over again. No wonder there was no childhood obesity back then—little girls were jumping through hoops for Chatty Cathy, one demanding hunk of rubberized plastic. At age five, I watched the commercials on our black-and-white Zenith in Kansas, not knowing that twenty-three years later I would not only meet Chatty Cathy but also marry her.

My future wife wound up a child television actress thanks to the confluence of geography, a persistent stage mother, and general cuteness. Their family lived in the San Fernando Valley town of Encino, which was crawling with A-listers. In my wife's cozy neighborhood, Judy Garland, Tim Conway, and Walt Disney all had houses, as did the biggest movie star of all time. One day on the grocery checkout line my future wife was making a typical five-year-old's demand for her mother to buy her a Hershey bar.

"Please, I want it!" she begged.

Standing her ground, her mother, Lillian, said no. The kid kept begging until some impatient man in line behind cleared his throat. The mother didn't need advice on how to deal with a screaming kid, so she turned to give the stink-eye to the man. The buttinsky was John Wayne.

"Give the little lady the candy, ma'am," the Duke directed.

The fear of insulting Hollywood royalty momentarily immobilized her, so he drove home his point by mouthing the word "Now." A candy purchase was immediately made.

Directly across the street from my wife's house lived the biggest TV stars in the world, Roy Rogers and Dale Evans. Monday through Friday they were shooting at rustlers and bad guys, but by Sunday morning they were always cleaned up for services at Saint Nicholas' Episcopal Church. A sign in Roy Rogers's front yard said BIENVENIDO, which translates "welcome," which they did every Tuesday afternoon, opening the front door to the neighborhood kids.

"Who wants to see Trigger?" Dale'd ask as the starstruck children filed by the most famous horse in the world. Trigger didn't mind the attention, but why would he? He was dead. When Trigger went to that big haystack in the sky, Roy and Dale had him stuffed and then placed him in their foyer. Maybe it became a neighborhood tradition, because when their neighbor Walt Disney passed away somebody apparently liked the idea of keeping Walt around, but they didn't stuff him and put him in the hall, they just cut off his head and put it in the deep freeze.

"Okay, kids, when I open the refrigerator door, look on the left, and you'll see the guy who invented EPCOT."

My wife's father, Joe, was a salesman for a New York–based lingerie company. When I eventually met him I admitted I was unfamiliar with that line of work, but he cleared it up by explaining, "I work in ladies' underpants."

My wife's mother, a onetime New York model, started reading the show business trades, finding open auditions, and putting the kids to work. Barely knee-high to a William Morris agent, they did commercials for cars, fast-food joints, hair color, you name it; when they smiled and held up the product, America bought it.

"You deserve a break today!" My future wife lip-synched Barry Manilow's jingle for McDonald's while looking really cute in a paper hat.

"Here, O. J." was her line when she tossed the Hertz keys to O. J. Simpson as he dashed through the concourse of the Palm Springs airport. Just think, had my future wife not given him the rental car keys, he might never have gotten back to Los Angeles, and American history could have been much different. Slow-speed chases are almost impossible unless the car is turned on.

Eventually she wound up at ESPN, as one of that network's first on-air women, and later at NBC in Washington, where I spotted her in the commissary and made it my life's mission to get a date with her. After a series of awkward encounters I eventually wore her down, for a mercy date. As I left her apartment that night I told her we'd be married. She presumed I was mentally unbalanced, but real life never lets you down—we were married five months later, and fourteen months after that, she was begging to have a word with the nurse who controlled her pain medicine as the real-life Chatty Cathy was about to birth a baby. Somebody please alert Mary Hart.

Back to that delivery day. After the hospital admission, she was escorted to a bleak labor room with very unflattering fluorescent lighting and changed into what they called a gown, but in reality, with the back side never fastened it was more of a labor and delivery apron. We asked what to expect, and they explained that sometimes a first-pregnancy delivery went fast, other times it dragged on, so to be on the safe side, her doctor was inducing the labor by injecting her with a potent mix of pharmaceuticals that would trigger some sort of hood release on her southernmost parts. That was the theory. However, the powerful drug Pitocin did nothing to her—she had some immunity to it, and instead we just sat there waiting. Think Amy Winehouse in stirrups.

"When should we start a college fund?" She sounded like a Morgan Stanley commercial.

"Why bother?" I said flippantly, unaware of the power of compound interest over twenty years; instead, I turned my attention momentarily to pressing matters. "Pass me the *People* magazine. I want to do the crossword."

A five-letter word that means "review word for a successful show"?

BOFFO I carefully printed perpendicular to *BORK,* waiting for nature to take its course. Killing time later, I walked past the nursery with all of the bassinets lined up in rows with screaming strangers, and at that moment I wondered what my parents had gone through on my birthday almost exactly thirty years earlier. Family historians remember my mother had contractions for thirty-six excruciating hours—a labor any longer and they'd have made her an honorary Teamster.

Eighteen months after my mom and dad's wedding and honeymoon in the Wisconsin Dells, where they memorialized their big trip by keeping every menu from every restaurant they visited, it was time for my world premiere. At two o'clock in the morning on October 19, my mother was in the delivery room of the town's only hospital when her attending physician made the shocking announcement that my birth was delayed because I was essentially stuck somewhere between the Panama and birth canals. My heart rate was slowing into the red zone, so the doctor quickly gave nature a helping hand and dragged me into this world with a set of stainless steel forceps that looked like jumbo salad tongs.

And where was my dad? He was not in the room, he was not in the state, he was not even in the country. Eight months before I was born my father had entertained a hard-to-resist employment opportunity. The job promised exciting travel, accommodations, and a fantastic new wardrobe if you liked camouflage. He was drafted. After a basic training that made sure he understood the correct end of a rifle to point at the bad guys, the army lickety-split dispatched him to Stuttgart, Germany, to make sure disgruntled Mercedes-Benz employees didn't take over the world on their lunch hours.

"Put down the cluster bomb, Dieter, and go rivet some diesels."

My father saw me for the first time when I was eighteen months old. Despite missing hundreds of diaper changes, crying jags, and a near deadly whooping cough, I was by his account still adorable.

The stern draft notice from the Pentagon was the reason my father was not in attendance for my birth, but back then few guys were in the delivery room for the actual birth. Generally men would drive their wives to the hospital, park the car, and wait for an announcement. Fast-forward a generation and I was not only in the same room with my wife, but I was her labor and delivery coach, having spent at least half a dozen evenings in various community center basements learning Lamaze breathing, to help my wife during the miracle of birth. Here's a news flash: that breathing is a scam. It doesn't work. I prompted Kathy to pant and blow exactly as we'd been taught, and yet during several raving intervals she informed me that it felt like she was trying to pass a DeLorean.

The cynic in me wonders whether the breathing exercises were developed by nurses and doctors who had grown tired of the expectant father asking "Is it time?" and wanted to give both the man and the woman something to do while they waited for the baby to squirt out. It did nothing to ease my wife's pain, but if it was simply a distraction to give her something to concentrate upon, may I suggest they abandon Lamaze and install a *Guitar Hero 3*. That way she has something with which to pass the time that'll distract her from her contractions, and if she can score seventy-five thousand points before the baby is born, she should get free parking.

Thirteen hours after our predawn arrival a nurse noticed that our baby's heartbeat had slowed down considerably, and there was some worry that he was stuck, which could mean the ultimate disaster: a lawsuit. A brief conversation in hushed tones and a flurry of activity as something was pulled out of a sterile drawer, and just as I was delivered three decades earlier, my son arrived courtesy of a set of giant salad tongs. Peter James, the most beautiful child the world had ever seen, made his debut with a handsome complexion the same color as Superman's hair, blue.

That event marked the *single greatest moment of my life*. My legacy weighed seven pounds eleven ounces and would have stood twenty-two inches tall if he'd been able to stand, which that first day I wasn't going to demand. The only thing he could do at that moment was lie there in a blue knit stocking cap like the neighborhood's youngest felon waiting to knock over a 7-Eleven.

"We'll just wrap him up like a tater and put him under the lamp," one of the reliable nurses said as she placed him under the cozy glow of what looked exactly like the heat bulb at McDonald's that keeps the fries warm; the only thing missing was the shaker of salt. Daydreaming about how my life had changed in that instant and how I finally had someone to watch wrestling with, I overheard the nurse querying the delivery team members, filling out his Apgar score, which I learned was how one evaluates a newborn's physical condition. The closer to ten, the better the score.

"He's a nine, very good," the nurse announced.

His first test, and already he's an A student! Later by the vending machines I met a new dad who proudly articulated his son's grade. "He's a seven," he bragged.

"That's a great score," I said, which was a lie. Already so far behind my son. I should have just told that father to forget about Harvard and send an early-admission application to Clown College.

There was a further wrinkle to our delivery day. One week earlier, a baby had been snatched at a suburban hospital, and now that we could stop being worried about a healthy baby, we could advance to nonstop parental hysteria and worry that our only child was about to be kidnapped by some slug of the earth who craved what we had, a Smurf-blue baby. Ergo we made a pact that our baby Peter James would stay the entire time in my wife's room and not the public nursery, which meant one of us would have to be awake around the clock eyeballing the baby. We did not consider ourselves paranoid, and the voices in my head reassured me of that, but my wife was positive a direct Bruno Hauptmann descendant was circulating nearby with a minivan and an extension ladder on the roof.

"You go home and get some rest," Kathy told me as I kissed my only legal tax deductions good-bye. Amped up on adrenaline, I intended to go directly to sleep, but I was too keyed up, so I started calling friends and family members to tell them the good news. First our parents, then our siblings, followed by miscellaneous family members, lifelong pals, our Lamaze coach, and finally people at work.

"What are you doing home? We need to celebrate," said one of my best friends who just like me also had a new son at home. My own father had told me that the night I was born, the guys from his army unit took him to one of Stuttgart's finest beer gardens and served up what they did best, a large hangover.

"I really can't, at six I'm on kidnapping duty," I told him, which seemed like an easy dodge, despite the feeling that made me want to celebrate the greatest day in my life.

"One drink," he pleaded. In fact, an adult beverage would actually help me relax. Besides, when a man wins an Oscar or the Super Bowl, do you think he goes home and falls asleep with the rich chocolate taste of Ovaltine?

"All right, but I've got to be home by midnight."

On the way to my house, he picked up my boss, who would give me political cover with my wife if she ever found out about my cocktail guzzling while she was standing shotgun over our son, the future president of the United States. For my extra-special single celebratory drink, my friends had selected a very popular spot, which I'd read was a watering hole for celebrities, lobbyists, U.S. senators and congressmen, and even the mayor of Washington.

"Let's go," my buddy announced as he and my boss handed the valet the keys. Suddenly paralyzed, I could not in good conscience party with my pals while the mother of my child was two miles away in a lonely semiprivate hospital room with bad lighting, strung out on intravenous drugs and delusional that the bogeyman was going to stop by after visiting hours. There was one other major reason I was uneasy getting out of the car: they'd brought me to a strip joint.

"I came here when my son was born," my friend divulged as he paid whatever it cost to see people naked. "When they find out you're a new dad, lap dances are half price!"

The way he said it, it sounded like an unbeatable deal for the value-conscious porn addict, which I was not. However, it was the end of a very long day, and while my wife rode the storm with the benefit of an epidural, I was thirsty, and there was absolutely positively no way she would ever find out. I thanked my boss for paying the cover, which I knew he'd eventually expense as a business lunch with the sports guy.

Inside it was very dark, and the music volume was set to *melt eardrums*. Aside from our new-father fiesta, there were guys at three or four other tables aimed in the direction of an abandoned stage. The waitress stopped by to take our drink order, an amiable girl who wore a junior college cheerleader uniform that was three sizes too tight and way past anything comfortable. The only one who could pull off wearing that size in public would be Polly Pocket.

"What are you drinking, guys?" she screamed over the music in a voice at a volume one would usually associate with an airplane evacuation.

Despite my plan to have a single highball, I was told there was a two-drink minimum, so I ordered a double vodka, which was actually a sensible selection as it was not only pure alcohol, but it could be used as an antiseptic, which could be useful in that disgusting hellhole of a club where a sane person would flush with his foot.

Just as the watered-down cocktails arrived I heard the police siren.

Uh-oh.

Simultaneously a door flew open and the room was filled with red flashing lights. My first time in a strip joint was the night of a police raid. Tomorrow the *Washington Post* would run a photo of me being led out with my hands over my face, under the headline "TV's Father of the Year," opposite a picture of my one-day-old boy being held by my future ex-wife, who'd been sitting up bug-eyed all night, with a frying pan in hand waiting for the evildoers to take our baby. From the perp-walk photo the new dad would appear to be sporting a skillet dent in the forehead.

When in mortal danger one either puts up one's dukes or runs. It's called fight or flight. I'm a flighter, opting for an immediate evacuation, and was surprised that my friends weren't ready to run. Instead, they were clapping—what were they, members of the Police Benevolent Association, happy the cops were about to take us downtown?

Scanning the room, I saw that nobody was leaving, and curiously, there were no uniformed officers in the room. The siren was actually the intro of an Ohio Players song, and the lights were just part of the show. No police. I was momentarily convinced that karma was punishing me for being there. Add my hyperactive imagination, fueled by exhaustion and straight vodka, and my mind played a funny trick on me. I had punked myself. Thankfully, that night at the strip joint there was no bust. Allow me to rephrase that—I didn't have to make bail.

In an ironic turn of events, the first performer was costumed as a registered nurse. Looking exactly like one of the two dozen angels of mercy I'd met that day, this Florence Nightingale was swinging a stethoscope à la Mae West's feather boa. What a multitasker—not only was she an exotic performer, but with her diagnostic equipment she could detect mitral valve prolapse.

As she tossed her hat with a big red cross on the front into the front row, and long before she was able to gyrate out of her hospital whites, I excused myself from the table, but my companions didn't care; they were, after all, devoted lovers of live theater.

Looking for the restroom, I found a deserted backroom saloon that had a couple pay phones and an odd feature for this type of business, a salad bar. Momentarily questioning who in his right mind would eat that stuff considering all of the germs and bacteria and belly button lint floating around, I spotted some of those little Chinese corns that have been a weakness of mine since college. Picking up a styrofoam plate and a plastic fork, I loaded it up with the second pair of salad tongs I'd seen that day.

It was delicious, but then again I was starving. I nonchalantly dined on a plate and a half of salad parts, and when I returned to the room the nurse was gone and a French maid was on the catwalk. I suspected this was a maid who did not do windows, but did everything else.

"I have got to go," I barked on my return, but my companions were oblivious. As I left to hail a cab, they remained visitors to Silicone Valley.

The next morning at six I was at the hospital, where I found my wife rocking our baby, her head twisted uncharacteristically to the left. I estimated she had a three-Tylenol stiff neck. "I haven't had a second of sleep and I'm dying for a bath," she said, carefully handing me the boy. "What did you do last night?"

"Not much, just headed home," I replied, which was technically true. I did go home, and I didn't do much else, unless you counted eating a salad teeming with E. *coli* in the back room of a notorious burlesque theater. Completely truthful, *to a point,* I had that same nauseous feeling one has after a Steven Seagal film fest.

Around noon our friend Tommy Jacamo from the Palm restaurant, where we'd gotten engaged, brought my wife a lobster that was exactly the same weight as my son, seven pounds eleven ounces, which at that place would have cost eighteen thousand dollars, plus parking. By the time the lobster carcass was sucked clean, I was helping the new mom remove the napkins I'd festooned around her neck when my friend whom I'd left at the strip joint twelve hours earlier materialized at her door with a wrapper full of grocery-store flowers. A lovely thought. He then sweetly offered an unparalleled compliment to a mother who'd just gone through over a dozen torturous hours of delivery and a sleepless night in a scary metropolitan trauma center.

"What's with the kid's hair? You're both blonds. He looks Cambodian."

A wonderful bedside manner. He was the kind of person who really needed sometimes to edit his conversation but did not, which was evidenced by the next thing to spill out of his yap trap.

"Did you tell her about the strip joint?"

"Strip joint?"

"He's kidding," I guffawed, knowing that he would instantly gauge from the nervous yet brazen tone of my voice that this was a third-rail topic that must be derailed at that exact moment.

"The fancy one up from the Safeway."

Luckily for him we were in a hospital, so in a few moments after I'd choked the life out of him and left his body near a Dumpster out back, somebody in a white coat could revive him, as long as he had a valid Blue Cross card in his pocket.

"Are you telling me . . ." I could tell by the tone of my wife's voice that this would be the mother of all butt chewings. "While I was here after fifteen hours of labor on the hottest day of the year staying conscious so nobody would kidnap our baby, *you were at a topless joint?"*

"It was bottomless, too," my soon-to-be ex-friend chimed in. "But he didn't stay for that."

What was he doing? Was this a hidden-camera segment for *Montel*? This must have been what it was like on that mountain with the Donner party at the moment they realized that they had limited buffet options. "If you're not using your fingers . . . can I snack on your index?"

An unhealthy period of quiet swept across the maternity ward as he tried to change the subject, rapping his fingernail on the side of the plastic see-through bassinet, trying to wake up our son. Luckily, our blue baby with the thick black hair was a very sound sleeper. Sensing that his work destroying our family was done, my friend left.

"She wasn't really mad, was she?" he asked a week later.

"Not at all," I snapped back as I stared at his rib cage, trying to use mind control to stop his beating heart. In reality, she was hurt, but she had a 7-pound baby to tend to, and a 170-pound bigger baby to train. For that next year, I always wondered whether she'd memorized Raoul Felder's 800 number, occasionally dialing it for practice.

While it's easy to become a dad, the simple act of a birth does not make you a father; that is something that is learned along the way. Intelligence does not equal wisdom. It's been twenty-some years since that night, and considering the emotional blowback, I can honestly say I have not been to a strip joint since, and I've got the single-dollar bills to prove it.

My friend was never invited to share the miracle of my two daughters' births. Mary was born on November 1, All Saints' Day, which I have a feeling God had a hand in. According to what I've read on Craigslist, that is one of the hardest days of the calendar year to book a lap dancer.

Our final child, Sally, was also born in July, and within an hour of her arrival, her brother, Peter, and sister, Mary, were in the room, singing "Happy Birthday." Mary was a typical three-year-old, mesmerized, paying rapt attention to the new baby for almost a minute, and then bored silly. She must have thought she was at a restaurant: "Me use potty?"

She excused herself to the private bath, and a few minutes later, after some suspicious giggling, the door swung open, and there she stood naked. We knew it was an attention-getting reaction to the new baby, but it was also really cute. That was around the time U.S. House Republicans had something called the Contract with America. "Look at the nudie," my wife said, laughing. "She's a regular *Nudie* Gingrich."

I automatically felt obligated to add to her joke. "And you know what Nudie Gingrich's Contract with America is . . . a chicken in every pot and a *pole* in every bedroom." My wife guffawed momentarily until she made the connection that this was not the first time her husband had been in the presence of a naked person on the birthday of one of their children.

Suddenly angry for the 19,300th time over the infamous strip joint incident of 1987, she launched into an uncomfortable recitation of the facts.

I am never going to live this down, I was thinking to myself, when a lightbulb went on over my head, and I realized that having your wife repeat the same thing over and over again is exactly what happens when a guy marries Chatty Cathy.

2

School

Don't Eat the Paste

During the early seventies there was a popular hit that seemed to be on our AM radio whenever Paul Harvey was not. Sonny Bono's then wife Cher sang:

"Gypsies, tramps and thieves . . ."

However, the first fifty times I heard it I could have sworn she was singing:

"Gypsies, tramps and <u>Steve's</u> . . ."

As a Steve myself, that got my attention, and suddenly I was hooked on the lyrical wisdom of Mrs. Bono.

"I was born in the wagon of a traveling show,
My mama used to dance for the money they'd throw. . . ."

Oddly, I felt a kinship to Cher, and her song was my anthem. *My* father was a traveling salesman, and by the time I was fourteen we had moved seven times. Nobody threw money at my mother, but she did dance whenever Johnny Mathis would sing on our Magnavox Astro-Sonic stereo. Once when I heard Cher starting that song on the car radio I said to my mom, "Listen, it's about us!" After one chorus Mom was wincing. I was an innocent second grader who didn't realize that the song was about a family where the father was a bootlegger and the mother was a hooker.

"Stephen James!" Mom started her song review. "We're not Gypsies or tramps, we're Swedish!"

Had our family been affluent I probably would have been shipped off to St. Xavier's School for Troubled Boys and Wayward Pets. She just shook her head; it was neither the time nor the place to explain ladies of the evening or something even more incomprehensible, Cher.

The fact that we moved around was challenging—just about the time I'd get to know a few kids, my father would get transferred to another territory, so I was the perpetual "new boy." My dad suggested I volunteer for various after-school events. When nobody else in Miss Perseghal's class would agree to appear as Christopher Columbus at a schoolwide assembly, I raised my hand, and soon I discovered why nobody else was interested in the part—a lengthy script had to be memorized and there was a costume. The school wardrobe mistress felt that Columbus was the ultimate swashbuckling adventurer who much like the host of *Dance Fever* should wear an extremely revealing pair of gold leotards. At one point during my single public performance I noticed a little giggling and immediately attributed it to my Italian accent, which was less Genoa and more Chef Boyardee. Slowly I shifted back to my normal speaking voice, but the twittering continued, so I paused for a moment to peer over my scroll and noticed that nobody was looking at my clown-sized funny hat as I'd imagined; instead, they were all checking out my shiny tights. Drawing the curtain on their peep show, I promptly lowered the scroll I was reading to below the belt level to conceal my southern hemisphere.

Luckily we moved later that year and I was at a little schoolhouse on the prairie that seemed like it came straight from an episode of *The Waltons*. It was an honest-to-goodness one-room schoolhouse, where every student regardless of age or class was in the same room. Three first graders, two second graders, one third grader, three fourth graders, and two sixth graders, eleven in all—it was a multiclass casserole. I was the oldest boy student stuck in a room with a bunch of little kids just at the time I was starting to notice the ladies. There was only one girl my age, cute as a bug and smart as a whip (back when bugs and whips mattered), and she was certainly girlfriend material, except for the overarching fact that my potential dream date and I shared a classroom with two of my sisters, who'd hang on every one of my dreamy glances in the direction of the girl in the training bra.

Flirty glances, however, were not allowed in the one-room schoolhouse. The staff made sure of that. We had a teacher, a principal, a nurse, a janitor, and a phys ed instructor, five people all jammed inside the five-foot two-inch frame of Mrs. Hazel Lloyd, a grandmotherly sixty-year-old career teacher who'd spend a portion of the morning with each student issuing various assignments, until 11:45 A.M., at which time she'd disappear.

"Let's go, children," she'd announce, and we'd file into another part of the school, where she'd be wearing an apron and a ridiculous hairnet so she could personally sling state-mandated starchy lunches. Before we'd adjourn for recess in the gym, where her high heels had left a thousand black scuff marks under the basketball hoop, she'd call us around the piano and we'd sing a song that the kids of all the ages knew, which meant it was usually about a dog or a cowboy, or the dog of a cowboy. Hazel Lloyd could do everything and knew everything in the world. She was like *Parade* magazine's Marilyn vos Savant, in sensible shoes.

She was the greatest educator I'd ever had, and I was sad to leave when it was time for junior high and high school. My only constant friend at both of those schools was my pal Alan Elsasser, a powerfully built athlete who convinced me after football to go out for the wrestling squad. The workouts were exhausting, and our opponents were literally bone breakers, but the traumatic part was that as a wrestler I was suddenly back in tights. A shade over six one, I wrestled in the 118-pound division. I was the boniest kid on the team. I was Kate Moss before Kate Moss.

One night after practice I was the last one in the shower and completely alone as I got cleaned up.

"Hey, Slim." I turned to see who was quietly standing behind me and was shocked to see not a teammate or coach, but a photographer from the school newspaper who an hour earlier had taken our official team photo. Why was he in the shower aiming a camera at me? I was naked!

Click.

"Don't worry, I don't have film in it." He grinned. Had I been wearing pants I might have walked over and inspected the camera, but I was bottomless and didn't feel like frisking the photographer, so I took him at his word. The next day twenty-five eight-by-ten black-and-white glossies of a very surprised skinny boy were taped to a single row of lockers near the school entrance. The entire student body was able to see my entire student body.

Rather than confronting the kid with the camera who took the shot—he was in fact twice my size—I pretended it never happened. I never told my family about being literally caught with my pants down. Of course if that happened today, if photos of a bare-naked minor were circulated at a public school, that place would be raided faster than you could say "Geraldo Rivera."

I sometimes wondered whether that episode was why I had a recurring dream of arriving for class amid a wail of laughter.

"What's so funny?" I'd demand to be let in on the joke.

"You came to school naked, again."

I had that dream for at least ten years after I graduated from college. Inexplicably, sometimes I dreamed I wasn't just nude, but sitting in a see-through aquarium being pushed through the school in a shopping cart. Eventually I just regarded it as some post-traumatic stress craziness and classified it as a dopey dream. Curiously, the worst part about showing up for school naked was no pockets— where does a guy keep his protractor?

Fast-forward a generation, and my wife and I made a pledge to try to keep our children from going through the school shabbiness we'd experienced. Because I'd lived in so many houses in so many towns, I made a vow to give our kids some stability and never move from our house, because we always wanted them to know exactly where home was.

There are few things harder for a parent than sending his or her five-year-old off to school, except maybe a colonoscopy, although they both require ample sedation. I was at work when our eldest went to school on the first day, so my wife chronicled it with photographs and videotape, and when she realized "They don't have seat belts on the bus!" she and the neighbor lady hopped in a chase vehicle and tailed the bus, "just to make sure it went to the right school" three blocks from our house.

While a parent's anxiety is palpable, our son, Peter, didn't wait for weeks or months to let his apprehension build to a crescendo. He freaked out the first day before lunch.

RRRRIIIINNNNGGGGGGGG!

"Who's in trouble?" my son asked his kindergarten teacher as she picked up a ringing egg timer. Peter sat there with the panicked look of somebody caught halfway down the sheet rope in a prison break.

"Nobody . . . yet," she said with a laugh, compounding his confusion. Some kids are terrified of Santa or, for good reason, clowns; Peter had a childhood fear of egg timers. Whenever his best friend Phil got in trouble, Phil's mother would twist an egg timer for an appropriate length of punishment and sentence the boy for that amount of time in the dreaded time-out chair. Name-calling got five minutes, wire fraud ten to twenty.

When my son heard the egg timer he assumed somebody was in trouble and about to be marched over to the time-out chair. His kindergarten teacher had decided that the class would color for exactly ten minutes, and to be precise she started an egg timer. My son was almost done with his coloring assignment when time ran out halfway through his blue period.

To her credit the teacher later diagnosed a little anxiety and called him up to her desk to talk privately. As she explained how the timer helped her manage time, he was half listening, half exploring the off-limits region of the teacher's desk. In particular his eye was drawn to a row of shiny cans stacked on shelves next to the story corner. After the timer talk he politely asked what the cans were, and she glanced over and said, "Oh, that's my special protection."

Unable to read the label, from one of his Berenstain Bears books he recognized a single word on a can: *net*. He then deduced as any five-year-old would that it was some sort of protective aerosol net from the labs of Spider-Man. Suddenly my son was panicked by the prospect of not finishing assignments on time—when the buzzer went off, the teacher would unholster a can and ensnare him in a liquid net and then drag him down to the principal's office, where he would be forced to sit in a corner until he could correctly name the state capital of Rhode Island.

"Rhode Island City?"

When he got home and was asked for a first-day review, he gave the teacher good marks, and then, over chicken-fried chicken, almost as an afterthought, he revealed, "She's got cans of protection."

Protection in a can?

Clearly his teacher had tear gas in class. Having promised I would not be one of those buttinsky dads, I followed my wife's sage advice not to complain immediately. Instead, I waited to voice my concerns at our first parent-teacher conference.

"Are you out of your mind having Mace around children?" I flat out told her thirty seconds after cooing, "So nice to meet you. Peter simply adores you."

"*Mace?*"

"Peter told me you have some sort of aerosolized weapon."

"I wouldn't even know where to buy Mace." She sounded so innocent, but don't they always, the superguilty?

Pitiful getting caught red-handed and then lying directly to me at our first face-to-face. As she yammered and stammered I looked over her shoulder momentarily and noticed a stuffed tiger just like the one my father had brought back from the army. It sat next to a shelf that had four gleaming cans of industrial-strength Aqua *Net*.

Protection in a can.

She wasn't packing poison gas; she had been talking about extra-super-hold unscented aerosol *protection for her hair*. Slowly my eyes returned to the teacher's head, and indeed she had an inflexible beehive that would surely remain in a fixed position during a subtropical cyclone.

"Mace, schmace," I blurted out, trying to change the subject. "The main thing I wanted to address is the egg timer."

She was surely relieved that I was no longer accusing her of warehousing a weapon of mass disruption, but I knew in my heart that she would forever quietly categorize me as some nut dad who spent nights listening to Art Bell on the radio while waiting for the day that scientists could perfect a robot wife that was affordable and reliable.

"I've always used it, but from now on, I'll make sure he knows the timer is about to ring, so it doesn't scare him." I was delighted to hear her say that, and true to her word, he was not petrified again during that year, when she went through enough hair spray to carve a quarter-mile-wide hole in the ozone over Helsinki.

The egg timer and Mace case illustrate how as a father I made it my job to protect my kids, regardless of reason. When I was in school my teacher asked my parents how they felt about in-class discipline, and my father told them it was okay with him to spank me if I was asking for it. How quaint. If a kid got a dose of discipline today with a school paddling, before the kid's butt cooled down, there certainly would be a caravan of live trucks outside the school and Shepard Smith demanding to know, "Was there screaming?"

Okay, so corporal punishment has been banned, but why has common sense also gone the way of the passenger pigeon?

"Excuse me," Sally asked her science teacher during a discussion on cloning. "Is it Dolly llama or Dolly the lamb?" An innocent question—she had a general idea that there was one of both; one was a cloned critter, the other a picture in Richard Gere's wallet.

"Miss Doocy, a public school is no place to poke fun at a religious leader like the Dalai Lama," the teacher said. "You're trying to be funny. I've seen your father, and you're a family of jokers."

For the record, we may be jokers, and we also have a riddler in the family, but when did every harmless ad-lib become a potential three-day suspension? The Dalai Lama versus Dolly the lamb scandal earned Sally some stern words from a humorless administrator, and her parents were paralyzed with fear that a notation of "religious intolerance" would be placed in her permanent record.

"Don't worry about that," the principal assured us, which only made us positive they'd already written those exact words in big red block letters across the top of her transcript, making it impossible that she'd ever be elected pope.

Pondering the ramifications of a tainted permanent record forever haunting a person with its litany of juvenile indiscretions chronicled for posterity, I took the ultimate step in coming face-to-face with my own checkered past.

"Hi. I'd like to get a copy of my permanent record," I told a woman who answered the phone for the Clay County Unified School District 379. I was prepared to demand access via the Freedom of Information Act, but the woman wasn't much of a stickler for bureaucracy, and within a week I was holding the much-feared repository of all bad acts from school, the grammar-school holy grail, my permanent record. The contents had been a mystery for three decades, and when I opened it I was instantly horrified. There they were—my pretty good grades, the total number of days I was absent, and *nothing else*. Where was the bad stuff? My single detention, turning the hall into a giant Slip 'N Slide, or the senior prank release of four chickens in the library. Where was the history of my hijinks?

The threat of the permanent record had always been a significant deterrent to keep us from doing something really stupid. "The permanent record is a myth from cartoons," my daughter Mary informed me, and she was correct.

"Whatever happened to that lady in the one-room schoolhouse?" my wife asked one night when we were watching *To Sir with Love,* about the inspirational teacher. "Did you ever tell her thanks?"

Embarrassed that she'd meant so much to me when I was younger and yet I'd said so little since, a few days later I dropped a three-pager in the mail. About a week later I got a letter in exactly the same penmanship I'd seen twenty years earlier. "Stephen," she wrote, "I saw you on television recently and the word *media* is plural, and you've been using it incorrectly." Although she was right, I was a little insulted that she was picking on me. But then I realized she was still teaching. "I know your parents are proud of your accomplishments, as I am. You have grown to be the kind of person of whom every parent and teacher dreams."

I am covered with the fingerprints of Mrs. Lloyd and other teachers as well, like Mr. Denny and Ms. Chesser, Mr. Booth and Miss Corwin. I went through the list of every teacher for every grade as I flew back for my twentieth high school reunion. Before the half-hour slide show that would feature before and after photos illustrating dramatic hair loss and weight gain, I was situated at the bar with my best friends Bill and Gary. With a few giggles the absolute two cutest girls from my graduating class, who never spoke to me in school, sauntered up with a copy of our yearbook. The blonde started thumbing through it to what I imagined would be a mortifying photo of me—there were six in that annual alone. She flipped to the very back and revealed a single black-and-white photo held in place by yellowed tape: an archival photograph of a stunned 118-pound freshman wrestler caught from the rear and buck naked.

I was momentarily dazed. The brunette spoke in a hushed tone as if it might be illegal for thirty-eight-year-olds to be in the possession of the same kind of shot you'd see today on an Abercrombie & Fitch shopping bag. She whispered, "Nice butt."

In appreciation of the compliment, I nodded, because when somebody's right, she's right.

3

Duty

Young Men in Uniform

Early I wanted to join the army like my father, but then I saw pictures of my uncle Phil in Korea and I wanted to be a marine, until I watched a movie where deeply tanned navy guys consumed beverages out of coconuts while native girls cooed nearby. Eventually I enlisted in the only paramilitary organization that would take a ten-year-old, the Boy Scouts of America.

I felt the urge to serve my country because the sixties were a scary time in America; college campuses were ablaze and the nation was at war. It was a time of free love and dope that could kill an elephant but not Keith Richards.

My father thought some marching and encamping would be good for me, so the second Tuesday each month he'd drive me after supper the five blocks to the University United Methodist Church at the corner of Santa Fe and Kirwin in Salina, Kansas. He'd watch me open the door, and then he'd wave good-bye as I descended the stairs into the world of scouting, where the motto was "Be prepared to sell stuff."

"All right, men," I remember my leader saying one night as he ginned up the crowd. "Let's get out there and sell this popcorn. It's a good product at a good price that's good for America!" And then we'd spontaneously burst into applause, as if we were listening to a Tony Robbins pep talk at Orville Redenbacher's world headquarters.

Some kids could count on their families to buy whatever the product was, but my family was always cash strapped, so I'd have to make cold calls to total strangers. We sold popcorn, candy, wrapping paper, (oddly) some wallpaper, lightbulbs, and once an artificial milk substitute from a Caribbean island that gave people intense abdominal pain. Back then nobody would have thought to sue the Scouts over any potential health hazards from shoddy products, because we were operating with the collective goodwill of a nation that believed it was buying things to finance our many good works. In fact, we were moving things that our ingenious leaders got by the gross at rock-bottom prices, resulting in a healthy profit margin. I have no doubt that if those guys were still Scout leaders, they'd have their boys selling cut-rate Botox and knock-off Kate Spade handbags.

For two years I was one of the troop's top salesmen, I had developed an irresistible sales pitch during our lightbulb promotion.

"Would you be interested in a three-way?"

An astonishingly high percentage answered in the affirmative before I would pull out my sales sheet, which detailed the exact specifications of our newfangled three-way intensity lightbulbs. While very successful, I never caught up to our leading salesman, who always beat me in total sales. I had no idea what he told customers, but I wouldn't be surprised if he said, "If you buy this wrapping paper, an orphan boy will finally get a much-needed Adam's apple."

Our many profits were used to finance our monthly campouts and annual summer camporee. Officially the Scouts' mission was to build young men who would be trustworthy, helpful, courteous, kind, blah, blah, blah. The real reason I joined was to be given carte blanche to do dangerous stuff involving loaded rifles and flying axes, which occurred only when responsible mothers were at least half a county away.

This is living, I thought as I carefully trained the business end of the gun on my paper target at the base of a twenty-foot dirt hill that was the only thing stopping this pack of boys from slaughtering a herd of Holsteins.

"What are you doing?" a Scout leader screamed at my friend Phillip, who had accidentally waved a .22 in the general direction of the quartermaster, who got us a good deal on a gross of linoleum tile squares. "If you kill somebody, I'm going to have to fill out a form, and I hate paperwork, so cut it out!"

The guns and canoes were the two best activities and made all of my door-to-door glad-handing worthwhile; the rest of the time we did things like learn how to tie clove hitches and bowlines. The Morse code seemed useless, as we weren't heading back to the telegraph days anytime soon, and learning semaphore was absolutely idiotic until we realized we could send dirty messages by flag. We were, however, not good at that.

"Andrew just told me to 'kiss his *a-d-d*'?"

"The *s* is tricky . . ."

Midway through our expedition they had a parents' day. When my mother asked where the ladies' room was located, my leader pointed in the direction of a ditch latrine. I thought she was going to cry. My father the army vet seemed satisfied that I was going two weeks without television while using toilet paper one sheet at a time.

"We had a tent like this in Germany," my dad said, entering the canvas accommodation I shared with a panicky kid whose delicate gastrointestinal tract never adjusted to fried Spam or Old Trapper jerky.

"You got a dog in here?" my dad asked, which made me giggle, and I pointed in the direction of my roommate, who was outside showing his parents the tomahawk he'd gotten stuck thirty feet high in a cottonwood tree which he had to either retrieve or replace.

My father was quick to notice that I seemed to be the only kid at the entire camporee without a cot. I'd never asked my parents for one because they'd already bought me a new sleeping bag that year, and I didn't want them spending more money on me.

"I'm fine. I'll be home in six days," I told my parents as they climbed back into their Galaxy 500 and went home. That night I developed an excruciating stiff neck for the sixth night in a row, so I wrapped my mess kit in a shirt and used it as an improvised pillow.

Early the next day we learned how to start a campfire without matches, and later we were exploding beetles with a magnifying glass when somebody called me out because I had a visitor. Walking to my tent, I wondered who it was—all of my friends were on the campout already. I pulled the canvas door back, and there, sitting down, was my father. *Uh-oh, somebody was dead.*

"Sears was open," he said as he swept his hand Carol Merrill–style the length of my new cot. "I got you the last one." The fact that he had spent thirty of his hard-earned bucks on this made me feel special but a little selfish because that meant somebody at home was going without something.

"Dad, you didn't have to—"

"Stephen"—he always called me that—"I couldn't sleep last night knowing you had your head on dirt while your roommate, Sir Gas-a-lot, had a cot."

My dad made a joke that accidentally rhymed. I gave him a hug, and as he walked back to his car, I suddenly felt like I'd drawn the card in Monopoly that said "Bank Error in Your Favor." That night for the first time I was elevated from the rock-hard prairie floor on my brand-new cot, but now I had something new to deal with: the overwhelming smell of canvas. I now had the freaky sensation that I was trapped in a circus tent. The noxious fumes worked their magic on me and knocked me out about the time the coyotes stopped howling.

Those are the things I remember most vividly about my years in uniform. When in the second grade my son, Peter, brought home a note from school about joining a Cub Scout den, I insisted he try it. Pete loved the idea of having a uniform and eating out of little cans of potted meat, but as I learned shortly, much had changed in the thirty years since I'd worn the neckerchief. Let's start with his den leader, a wonderful woman whom we shall call "Mrs. Cuomo" because it was her name. She was a warm and engaging woman. But *she was not a man.* Sure, she could sauté and puree various traditional Italian family recipes and sew curtains with impossibly straight seams, but what could she possibly teach these young men about ax handling and fish gutting?

"Dad, she's real nice," Peter told me as I bit my tongue, knowing from personal experience that if a mother was present, no boy would ever take part in a longest, most disgusting belch contest. Mrs. Cuomo wasn't the only one. There were other nonmen.

"Nobody carves a pumpkin," a volunteer mom warned us, "until every father signs a waiver." She had prepared a quasi-legal document, handwritten on college-ruled three-ring-binder paper. It clearly stated that any injury incurred at her home would be the fault of the person with the knife, and not of the mother who made those knives available from her cutlery drawer. What had scouting come to? What had happened to the days when a boy and his dad could sit in the middle of the garage floor and carve gruesome jack-o'-lanterns while slicing off as many personal extremities as they wanted?

"I'm not losing my house if you lose a finger!" she said as I briefly contemplated giving her one.

My wife, Kathy, also got in on the action; whenever Peter would earn a merit badge or change rank, she would be charged with sewing it onto his uniform. Much of America had since abandoned home sewing machines, so she'd stitch the thick rubber and cloth badges on by hand. Just to puncture a needle through the patch was an arduous chore. She'd labor over a merit badge for an hour and was never satisfied by the end result, which seemed lopsided or crooked, but you didn't hear that from me.

When she asked one of the other mothers her secret she was told that everybody took the uniforms to a local tailor, who'd charge twenty dollars a badge. "You've got to be kidding me." On principle we never paid to have anything sewn on a uniform. Peter, on the other hand, was just so proud to be a Scout, he didn't care that his bear badge was stapled to his shirt.

While much of the Boy Scout program had changed and was now infiltrated by women, one annual event remained predominantly male: the pinewood derby. When I was a kid the Scout leader would hand everybody a cardboard box that had a long hunk of white pine, four silver nails, and a set of four black plastic wheels. My dad and I would talk extensively for about ten seconds and then he'd carve on it and then weight it with his Pitney Bowes postage meter until it was close to the maximum limit.

On race day, boys and their dads congregated in the church basement, where you could instantly gauge who had assisted in the construction of the cars. Most were done by Dad, but others were positively primitive because they were built by the boys themselves or in some cases with the help of their mothers, who were good with an iron but iffy with a coping saw. Just before my first derby race my father asked if he could make a final inspection of my car. He flipped its wheels up and squirted a little gray goo around the wheels.

"What's that?"

"Graphite," he said in the same hushed tone you'd use while purchasing performance-enhancing steroids at the Summer Olympics.

"What does it do?" I hushed along.

"Reduces friction."

I had never heard of graphite, but I could tell that if he was whispering and squirting it in the wheels after the car had been eyeballed by the judges, there was a chance this was taboo. I had the feeling that in a moment an official in kneesocks and with pasty white legs would disqualify me, and I'd feel the same kind of shame my friend Ted felt when his grandmother with glaucoma used her medical marijuana for brownies at a church bazaar. They sold out at fifty bucks a pan before the police arrived.

"Hi, Mr. Doocy," my friend Curtis said as he walked up moments after my car got juiced.

"Hi, Curtis. Where's your dad?" I asked.

"He had to work." His father was a delivery driver who had very long hours, which explained why his car was little more than the original hunk of wood with the wheels pounded into the sides and a number 7 hand scrawled on the side in ballpoint pen.

"Good job on your car," my dad said, in a way that I could tell he really meant it.

"Curtis, let me see your racer." My father was whispering again. "Is it okay if I lube up your wheels a little?" Curtis nodded, and four short squirts of the magic powder went directly into his wheel wells. I felt so proud of my dad, who was sharing our secret weapon with my pal.

"Third race, cars on the ramp," the Scout leader announced. Curtis, my friend Chris, and I carefully installed our racers at the top of the twenty-foot track.

"Three, two, one, race!"

A lever was thrown that let the cars freewheel down the plywood. The whole race took less than five seconds: the winner, by a substantial margin, was the unpainted car with the number 7 on the side. Yes, thanks to my father's generous offer of a friction-reducing squirt of graphite, my best friend, Curtis, beat me by a mile.

For many years people have mulled over what really happened that day in Dallas in 1963, what they found at Roswell; in my head I've pondered, Would Curtis have won without my father's help?

When my own son asked for help with his wooden car I discovered that just like the recruitment of women into the ranks of the Boy Scouts, the craft world had modernized the pinewood derby industry, and a shockingly wide array of stuff was now available on the Internet. Precarved car bodies, special 1.8-gram wheels, and "synthetic weight" to give the car that the kid didn't carve enough critical mass to win the race. If a parent was going to forgo the carving and sanding and painting part, and just buy a premade car, why not buy a trophy?

"We're doing ours the old-fashioned way," I told my son as I almost instantly gouged a Stanley carving tool about a half inch into my thumb. The blood loss was immediate and made a bloody blotch that was impossible to sand out of the surface of his vehicle.

"Can I try to carve a little?" Peter asked.

"Let Daddy do it. I'm old and don't need all of my fingers."

Our car was complete after three hours and one knuckle Band-Aid. A week later in the middle-school cafeteria it was derby day. Peter walked around with his car in a shoe box to minimize the chance that he would knock the front end out of alignment. Many cars were like ours: classics carved by father and son. But there were a number that looked like they were made from the same material usually reserved for NASA's Saturn exploration vehicles, stamped out by a computer, airbrushed, and even lacquered by a professional in Taiwan—they were works of art. If this had been an egg competition, their prefab cars were Fabergé, ours deviled.

As I waited for Peter's heat, I thought back to my own childhood victory stolen because of my father's kindness. But this was New Jersey, where they don't allow random acts of kindness—they're stopped at the Pennsylvania state line.

"Peter, let me see your car."

I eyeballed the immediate vicinity and, seeing we were alone, knew that I could slather our wheels in graphite and not have to share it with any of the other racers under any circumstances. So I started.

"Hey, Peter!" one of my son's den mates shouted halfway across the room as he lunged our way. "What's that stuff?"

Déjà vu all over again.

"Just a little Jiffy Lube," I said. "And it looks like we just ran out." Liar, liar, Dad's pants on fire.

"Mr. Doocy, my father says that graphite doesn't work as well as this," he said, pulling out a platinum tube of Extreme Graphite/Moly Dry Lubricant. "Do you want to try some?"

It was tempting. That kid was holding in his hand the Excalibur-grade material that you could only get online from Mexico, which is of course the world leader in dry lubricant.

"We're okay." And we were. We had a lot of fun doing the project together, despite that single loud word shouted when, pre-race, Peter dropped his car in the parking lot and his front right wheel broke off and rolled under our SUV. That was probably why the car finished dead last, a family tradition.

While we never won a trophy for a race car, Peter did win three consecutive blue ribbons for pumpkin carving. What can I say, we're half Gypsy and we're good with knives. He also received an award for salesmanship (we bought his entire stock), and once again to illustrate how times had changed, his award was a wooden plaque with an arrow on top, but there was no tip on the arrow so nobody would poke out an eye.

"Nobody gets an authentic, dangerous award until you sign a waiver."

While a lot had changed since I wore the neckerchief, the changes to scouting were probably a good thing, including the woman thing. The older I get, the more I realize that I should cut the cord to the past and embrace change. If Rick James could go from "Super Freak" to Old Navy, I should be able to switch from three-ways to extreme graphite dry lubricant.

4

Trouble

Fatherhood Is Hard—Get a Helmet

ate one afternoon Grandma and I were watching a soap opera called *The Secret Storm,* which seemed to be the dumbest name in the history of television because there was never a storm of any kind, no tornadoes, no hurricanes, no deadly wind chill, nothing. But Grandma Sharp liked it and she was our afternoon caretaker when my mom was working, so I'd sit and watch with her in the highly unlikely event that a vicious squall swept through and savaged everybody including that off-camera organist who had a habit of waking up and going to work just ten seconds before a commercial.

The word *Grandma* was hard for me to enunciate, and for a while it came out "Gunga," which became a lifelong nickname that stuck. Gunga was a full-blooded Swede, who worked odd nights as a short-order cook. She also had a great racket on the side: her friends at the federal government sent her something called Social Security—it was money simply for being old. She was my only blood relative who'd give us candy immediately before and after meals, and on birthdays and Christmas she'd open her seemingly bottomless purse to buy us the presents my parents refused, the ones with sharp edges or small swallowable parts, or that were simply dangerous.

"Look, it's a real gun *with a bayonet!*" I squealed on my fifth birthday, wondering where Gunga got it. Apparently she had met a guy at the diner who got her a deal on it despite the serial numbers being filed off, and I was able to keep it in my possession for almost a minute.

"Stephen James!" my mother snapped. "Put that gun back in the box! And Mother, please don't arm my children. They'll have guns when they're drafted." Another reason to hurry up and turn eighteen—I'd have army clothes and guns.

It was always midway through *The Secret Storm* that my mom appeared at the front door after work, and on that day she dropped a carton of Camels on the table and said, "Let's go, kids!"

My oldest sister, Cathy, was almost two and a wobbly walker, so I grabbed her hand and guided her off the porch, around the front of the car, and over to the passenger side, where I pulled open the big Ford's icebox-sized door. We always rode in what at that time was considered the safest spot of the vehicle, on the front seat; that way, in the event of an accident, my sister and I would be shot projectile style out the windshield like a couple of blond mortars.

Mom saw we were safely beside her so she put it in reverse, stared in the side rearview, and started to back down the driveway. Grandma materialized at the door and waved good-bye. "See you tomorrow."

"Okay, bye!" I yelled.

Cathy had been with Grandma less than thirty seconds earlier, but hearing Gunga's voice she made a typical two-year-old's snap decision that she'd rather stay there than go to our house and watch Mommy cook. The concept of MOVING CAR + SMALL CHILD = DANGER was beyond her years, and when she pulled up on the door lever it opened and she promptly fell out of the car. My mother, who was looking over her left shoulder away from us, missed it. But we both felt the front of the car bounce a little.

"JoAnne!" Grandma screamed in a bloody-murder voice I'd never heard on earth before and haven't since.

My mother turned around only when Gunga screamed. She immediately knew something bad had happened.

"Where's your sister?"

"She fell out, that way." I pointed toward the door.

"Oh my goodness!" Out she leaped, leaving me alone where I couldn't see a thing, until my mother appeared at the back passenger door with my screaming sister in her arms. "Mother, you drive." And Grandma got behind the wheel. We had never driven that fast through downtown as we headed south down the main drag toward the hospital. I rode up front, hugging the seat and looking back at my sister. I was the only one with no tears in his eyes.

"She'll be fine, Stephen, don't worry."

I wasn't worried at all, because this was nothing new. My sister was always falling down and then crying, although I couldn't understand why this time we were going to the hospital. As we pulled in, Gunga laid on the horn and somebody from the emergency room ran out with a gurney and they carted off my sister with Mom alongside as Grandma parked the car and we sat vigil in the waiting room.

Since I was a kid, nobody told me anything, so Grandma and I just sat in the waiting room, waiting. It was my first real hospital visit and nothing like *Medical Center* with Chad Everett, where doctors were urgently barking out orders to "Give them ten cc's, *STAT*!" as nurses set up IVs for somebody with a rare but untreatable disease that would somehow be cured one minute before an exciting preview of next week's episode. In real life there was no dashing, no running, just a whole lot of sitting and waiting with Grandma next to the pay phone as she chain-smoked Camels. The waiting-room TV was not tuned to the channel Gunga and I normally watched, so the shows that were playing were unfamiliar to me. We watched Merv Griffin and his distinguished sidekick, a slender and sophisticated man who sounded like he needed more fiber in his diet.

"Is that the king of England?" I asked her, pointing at Arthur Treacher.

"Looks like Orville Bebbemeyer from over in Brit," she said, reducing the Edwardian actor to a small-town hoaxer who'd affected a phony accent to one day franchise fried fish to a nation.

Grandma had been trying to locate my father all afternoon, but with no cell phone or answering machine, every fifteen minutes she'd walk over to the pay phone, dial our number, and wait for my father to answer, which he finally did around seven thirty that night.

"We're at the hospital—JoAnne ran over Cathy. Come quick."

That was the first time I heard officially that my mother ran over my sister. Within ten minutes my dad appeared at the double automatic door, and I remember a feeling of relief that now everything would be okay.

"The tire went right over her belly," Grandma told him, "and the doctor said because her bones are still so rubbery, nothing got broken. JoAnne's still in there with her."

"I could use a cigarette," Dad said as he turned to a passing physician from whom he bummed a Lucky Strike. He smoked it next to the nurses' station, where there were plenty of ashtrays right under an advisory from the surgeon general that cigarette smoking could lead to burning down your house. Why was the whole country worried about harmless smoke, I wondered, when the real danger to America was children falling out of cars only to be run over by their parents?

Miraculously, my sister had no internal bleeding and was going to be fine. Very late that night my mom told my dad to take me home. For the first time in my life, it was just the two of us alone in the house, sitting at the kitchen table as he drank one cup of coffee after another. I remember the pin-drop quiet framed something he said that was so remarkable to my five-year-old mind that I've never forgotten.

"Stephen, I wish I could trade places with your sister."

To me, that was just plain weird—why would my dad want to fall out of the car and have Mom run over him? Then we'd have two in the hospital, and with Mom sitting vigil, who would make my breakfast? I just nodded, and hoped his crazy idea did not come to pass.

Two days later my sister celebrated her birthday in the pediatric wing, where the staff threw her a party with chocolate cake and rubber gloves inflated balloon style. After many hugs and kisses, and a ride in a real wheelchair, Cathy was dismissed, and considering what had happened to her in the previous four days, she was lucky to be alive. But I wasn't thinking about my sister. I was fixating on the wheelchair ride and blown-up-glove balloons. I made a mental note to make sure my appendix burst mid-October so I too could have a bedpan birthday.

"Let's go!" my father said as he helped my mom and sister into the car. "JoAnne, I'm driving so nobody gets run over on the way home," he cracked, which got an audible gasp from Gunga and a dirty look from my mom, who surely felt guilty. Now I wonder if my father felt responsible that he wasn't at home the day it happened. He went through a period as a helicopter parent, hovering over us all the time, but eventually we broke free from him and resumed pulling bone-headed stunts that were at the danger level of the stupid chart.

When my own children came along, I thought about what my father had said, about how he would have traded places with one of his kids so she wouldn't have to suffer. It was a gallant and admirable suggestion, but I just didn't feel the same way. Maybe it was because all of my children's maladies were so pedestrian—why would I want to trade places with a kid with the croup?

Our children Mary and Peter did something that freaked us out in their first few months—their eyes would float around every which way. Thankfully, they grew out of it. At four months Sally's eyes were still randomly drifting around to the point that sometimes when you looked at her eye all you could see was white because her blue iris had rolled out of sight. She did not outgrow it, so my worried wife took her to a series of experts whose early treatment was to build up her eye muscles by putting a patch over her best eye.

"What's with the little pirate?" an older man who stopped at our garage sale said.

Not funny to us. We just icily stared at him as he bought an eight-year-old Sony Betamax for ten dollars. Had he not made the pirate crack I would have told him the only thing that worked on the Sony was the clock.

The eye patches didn't work, and before she was a year old Sally was already wearing glasses, which would stay on the bridge of her nose between five and nine seconds before she'd paw them off. To train her to keep her glasses on, they had my wife put Sally's hands in mittens, which got odd glares from strangers in mid-July when she was wearing them at the mall. She had a bright red pair, which when worn with her glasses and eye patch would have prompted the guy at the garage sale to ask, "What's with the lobster pirate?"

She could not see well, and as her vision deteriorated, her parents were constantly tormenting her with patches and mittens and glasses and burning eyedrops that blurred her sight so badly she'd crawl blindly every which way until she'd run into a wall headfirst. Sally had a truly pitiful start to life. One night before bed, I was giving her a bath and as I rinsed her hair I noticed a lump behind her left ear. I called in my wife, who'd never noticed it either. The next day we were blown away when we were told Sally would need brain surgery just when her eye doctor said she needed her eyes operated upon as well. Before her second birthday she would have two operations; curiously, she was at exactly the same age as my sister when she fell out of the car.

"I'll bring you back to recovery as soon as she's out," the nurse said, prying Sally from my arms. The child had sensed that this was no ordinary trip to the doctor, and alerted the entire first floor of the Fairfax County Hospital that she did not want whatever was waiting for her behind door number one.

Kidnappings are quieter. Every head turned our way, but nobody gave us the *shut up your kid* look, because they all recognized *that cry,* and at that moment not a soul wanted to be in our shoes. The sobbing was as loud and heartbreaking as I'd ever heard. Tears were streaming down my wife's face as the nurse carried the squirming Sally out of the waiting room through the automatic doors. We sat there stunned because our littlest, most vulnerable one had just been pried away by a total stranger and taken somewhere very bright and scary. In fact, we knew exactly where she'd been taken, because even though she was somewhere in a pre-op room three or four closed

doors away from us, we could still hear her screaming. It was a
wretched wail that went on for an agonizing ten minutes.

"That's not good," Kathy said as it abruptly got louder. We turned
toward the operating-room door, and our nurse was speed-walking
in our direction.

"We need a pacifier," she said sternly. "And a bottle. She's quite
disruptive."

I was surprised a state-of-the-art medical facility didn't have
standby generic pacifiers at the ready. Kathy dug the requested
items out of the diaper bag, and ninety seconds later Sally was quiet.
Relieved, we sat there scared out of our wits: what were they doing
to our baby in the operating room? It was then that I had my first
conversation as a parent with the Almighty. As a kid I'd had many urgent one-way chats, generally along the lines of "Now I lay me down
to rest, I hope I pass tomorrow's test. If I should die before I wake,
that's one less math test I have to take."

God never let me down. But this was different. I wasn't praying
for myself; it was somebody else who needed some help. I was new
at asking for third-party miracles, so I kept it simple. Because it was
an off-the-record prayer just between me and Him, I'd like to keep
it private, but it was exactly what you would expect from a father
whose child was on an operating table.

Of course we are an instant-gratification society, and when we
ask for things, we want an immediate return phone call, so I waited
for a sign that He was on the case. There was no deep James Earl
Jones voice that told me to relax, nor a friendly apparition on the
waiting-room TV that I could imagine was directed at me, or even a
pronouncement that I should go and build a baseball diamond in our
cornfield; instead, I felt an unnatural calmness because I knew she
had the best doctors in the world and it was now in God's big hands.

"Doocy family," the nurse barked out, walking through the automatic door. "Everything went well. She's fine." That was our cue to
start breathing again. Outfitted in hospital scrubs, we were led to a
blindingly bright recovery room, where Sally was breathing heavily

as she lay there hooked up to an IV and heart monitor in a cheerless little crib. It wasn't like her bed at home, no stuffed animals or mobile, no brightly colored sheets and matching bumpers—everything was simple and white. It was like a layout from Pottery Barn's hospital collection.

We were surprised that her eyes weren't bandaged over, and the doctor explained: "She'd just rip them off, so why bother?" A few quiet minutes after we arrived she started to stir, and when she opened her eyes they were instantly and recognizably straighter. Thank you, God. It was a medical miracle.

Her ten seconds of quiet time abruptly ended when she recognized us as the people who had sent her into the back room where those strangers in surgical masks had done things to her eyes. As she screeched I saw something I'd never witnessed in forty years on this earth. There was blood running down her face. She had *bloody tears*.

She looked like she'd just been punched in the eyes. This was easily the most pitiful thing I'd ever seen. We felt helpless. I held her tight on my lap as my wife caressed her hair. Late in the afternoon Sally's doctor released her, so we took her home, where she crawled over to her brother and sister and put her face next to theirs because she wanted no part of her parents.

At some point in the ordeal I thought back to my father, who'd said he'd change places with my sister who'd been run over, and I wondered, would I do the same? Would I trade places with Sally? My heart said yes, but as I thought of having a highly trained specialist prop my eyelids open with surgical toothpicks and then, using a razor-sharp scalpel, slice into the muscles behind the eyeball to make them an iota longer, I equivocated. Would I trade places with my child if it meant a doctor would poke me in the eye with a knife? The answer was swift and blunt—I would . . . but I just can't.

I had a really good reason: *because it was impossible.* Hiring a stand-in for surgery didn't make the sick one any better. In reality, all parents can do is hold our kids and stay with them until the pain or the scare goes away. Would I donate a kidney to my kid? Absolutely.

Retina, part of my liver? Yes and yes. If I've got some spare part, it's here for the taking, and that is a pledge that will stand as long as I'm standing.

On the day of Sally's brain operation there was some good news and some bad news. The good news was that the bump behind her ear was an unexplainable growth that had no effect whatsoever on her, so the brain surgeon simply removed it, and then vacuumed clean our insurance company.

"Thank goodness," my wife said to me while we were gathering our belongings in the waiting room. Then I noticed an important business bulletin had interrupted *Wheel of Fortune*. We watched live as Bill Gates, the world's richest man, signed papers to buy the television network where I worked. How would that affect me? They would clean house, and I would be fired tomorrow because my week hadn't been quite lousy enough.

I was so numb and bone-grindingly tired that I really didn't care. My father had taught me that jobs were simply places to go to make money for our families. My daughter was going to recover, and that was all that mattered. As for Bill Gates, if I ever saw his car in the parking lot I would probably steal his NERDMOGUL license plate and put it in Sally's room.

I am a father who would do anything for his family, and while Bill Gates is probably also a good dad who has made trillions with Microsoft, the truth is, I can shred his high score on Tetris.

5

Legacy

Should I Follow Tom or Diane Sawyer?

om Sawyer was the Million Dollar Movie my dad and I were watching when he pointed to the star's raft and revealed, "I built one of those." My father had chronicled much of his childhood, but the raft thing was tantalizingly new information. My immediate reaction was that if my father had done it, I should do it too. Some families from one generation to the next hand down heirloom jewelry, odd parcels of real estate, or gravy recipes; I would follow in my father's footsteps and make raft building our family tradition. Additionally, the idea of my own personal watercraft would put me on par with Ari Onassis, the Greek shipping magnate who was at that time married to Jackie Kennedy, the former first lady, and pictures of the two of them gallivanting on his yacht seemed to make the covers of every supermarket tabloid my mother bought.

Why'd the pretty lady marry the guy with the gut? I'd wonder years before I learned he was worth three-quarters of a gazillion dollars, and as I now know, vast wealth is very slimming.

My father gave me permission and a pile of unused lumber to set up a dry dock in the basement of our ranch house on Margaret Street in Russell, Kansas. A third-generation do-it-yourselfer, I used what I'd observed in the movie as the inspiration and general concept for the raft. There was one gigantic problem with me building that thing: I was only seven years old. As I look back, the State of Kansas Department of Transportation should have come to our house and arrested my dad on the spot because having a second grader build a watercraft clearly fell into the category of unwise things that should never be attempted, like singing karaoke sober.

I cobbled together as simple a flatboat as you could imagine, a wooden platform on a couple of two-by-fours. This was the first time I'd ever constructed something from scratch, and my father had encouraged me to add some extras. I chose something neither my father nor Tom Sawyer had on his raft: a steering wheel. That would make it much easier for me to navigate around partially submerged tree stumps as I spent lazy afternoons floating downstream. When I turned the primitive wheel side to side nothing happened. It wasn't hooked to anything and didn't really work, because a seven-year-old with a hammer has the mechanical wherewithal of a raccoon.

With the assembly complete, it was time for the final flourishes. I plugged my wood-burning iron into a basement plug and waited twenty seconds for it to heat up to nine thousand degrees, then branded the boat with a name that would surely be the envy of every second-grade boy: *Kon Stinki*.

During the final construction phase the excitement of my project had spilled over into a conversation with some school chums, who a few days later dropped by unannounced for a viewing. I wasn't ready to officially unveil it, so I did the adult thing and hid behind the water heater pretending I wasn't home. But my grandma was and told them to take a peek in the basement window. When I heard giggling, I assumed it was "That is so cool" laughter, but it was followed by "And look at that dorky steering wheel!" Another added, "Idiot," as they adjourned to spread more goodwill around the neighborhood and doubtless torture a cat with a red-hot poker.

For the first time in my young life I felt absolute humiliation. Getting your pants pulled down between classes was one thing, but this was personal. It was my own creation—why didn't they understand that? Rejected, dejected, and generally feeling rotten, I mothballed the project. My father arrived home in time to watch the final fifteen minutes of *The Mike Douglas Show,* but my mom confided what had happened and he went directly to the basement, where I was using a pry bar to rip the pine plank captain's chair out of the SS *Laughingstock*.

"Whatcha doing?"

I told him I'd decided not to finish it, because it was a stupid idea.

"Lemme see that hammer," he said, and in that magic dad way, he helped me put things back together on my raft and in my heart. "It looks seaworthy to me. Let's plunk it in water."

Instantly I forgot my previous heartbreak and started planning the maiden voyage. Lazy rivers are in short supply in western Kansas, but there are plenty of cow ponds, and my dad secured permission from one of his farmer friends to float my boat. When we arrived I personally thanked the landowner for the use of his lagoon, and I quickly discovered why my father nicknamed him Van Gogh—the man could talk your ear off.

Van Gogh, my dad, and I carried the raft from the trunk of my father's T-bird down to the water's edge. I just listened as the chatty farmer in the OshKosh overalls said things like "You can't milk a donkey if you don't have a pail."

Climbing into the captain's chair, I firmly gripped my faux steering wheel as my father and the farmer pushed it across the muck into the pond. It was a flawless launch, until the raft sank.

Not expecting a dunking, I was grossed out beyond belief, having just sucked the brown water from the cattle watering hole down my mouth and nose. My immediate damage assessment was that I'd sprung a leak, because that's how a second grader thinks, but in reality there was nothing to leak. It was supposed to float because that's what wood does—I simply needed more wood.

"My first raft sank too," my father lied. "Let's tell Mom we hit an iceberg."

The farmer, my father, and I dragged the shipwreck from the muck and mire and brought it high enough up the bank to keep it from being a cow hazard. The last thing I remember Van Gogh saying after abandoning ship was "You can put wings on a sheep, but it's still not a duck."

I'd loved the idea of building a raft as my father had, but there was a reason the world didn't use that form of water travel anymore: it was tricky and dangerous, and the widespread construction of rafts was most certainly best left to disgruntled Cubans.

From that day I became leery of any rituals from bygone eras that might have been popular once but, given advancements in science and recreation, were hopelessly outdated. "Don't make any plans for Saturday—I've signed you up for the father-son fishing derby," my wife informed me a generation later. Another time-consuming and quasi-dangerous throwback to the golden days, but my wife convinced me that if I didn't give my son a taste of some he-man activities, he'd wind up an adult child with few pastimes aside from folding cloth napkins into rabbits and hats.

When I was his age I loved to fish; my grandmother and I would spend hours on the banks of the Upper Des Moines, waiting for a nibble. I don't know if she really liked the sport or just wanted to chain-smoke Camels. My father was in charge of our bait. The night before a fishing expedition, Dad would turn on the garden hose and soak the grass, and presto, half an hour later, we'd go outside with flashlights and simply pick up the night crawlers that were luxuriating on the cool damp grass. These gargantuan worms were so big that if the fish didn't bite at them, one could just punch a carp and knock it out cold.

When my wife signed me up for the fishing derby, we were living where king-size worms were in short supply. Plus, I was always iffy about using a spade in New Jersey. "It's okay, kids, it's only Hoffa's toe."

I tried my father's hose trick, but Jersey worms have an attitude and won't come out of their holes for water unless it's San Pellegrino. Instead, I'd have to actually dig down into our garden to locate one. How does grass grow on concrete? I wondered after I turned over about two Advils' worth of dirt before I laid hands on half a worm, seconds after my shovel performed an accidental wormectomy.

"Pick him up, Peter."

"Him?" My son was horrified that our bait had a gender. I reminded him that there were trophies involved, and he promptly deposited the mortally wounded half worm in our bait bucket.

"Daddy, where are the fish?" was asked so many times in the derby's first hour that at one point I turned to see if my son had recorded that query and was playing back a tape. I knew the problem was our lure: the bait had croaked on the way to the fishing derby.

"Peter, look over there in those cattails for another worm." Ten minutes later he returned with a real squirmy one that he insisted he put on the hook himself.

"Good job, Pete!" I said loudly enough for the father and son next to us to hear. They had demoralized us many times that morning because each time they hooked a tiny sun perch, they yelped as if they'd just reeled in another great white.

"Be careful, that hook is sharp," I reminded as he struggled to pierce the razor-sharp curve through the worm's hind end. It was at that time that I first noticed the critter's distinctive markings and coloring.

"Peter, drop that thing! It's not a worm, it's a live baby water moccasin!"

We don't know who got the trophies, because we were in the emergency room making sure he'd not been injected with whatever factory-installed poison water moccasins have at the ready. In the waiting room I reminded myself that fishing, just like raft building, was an antiquated and dangerous leisure-time activity. Why would anyone subject himself to possible West Nile infection standing downstream from a leaking sewage-treatment plant? More to the point, why do people still fish today, especially if we've got Mrs. Paul out there somewhere reeling in the tilapia?

That was the last time we took our lives into our hands and went into the woods. I'd like to think it was from the fishing, but I think my son freaked out after I walked in and saw him watching *Deliverance*. The closest we've since been to a campout was during an electrical storm that knocked out the power to our neighborhood grid and forced the family to gather around a hurricane lamp in the living room. The thunder in the background provided the perfect atmosphere for ghost stories. The kids had never heard the one about the couple on lovers' lane who heard the radio bulletin about the guy with the hook for a hand who'd escaped from the mental hospital, and when they heard scratching on the side of the car they drove home, only to find the hook hanging on the door handle. I had goose bumps on my arms telling it.

"Dad, I saw that on an after-school special."

An undaunted terror master, I moved on and explained how my father had built me a tree house when I was in fourth grade and I'd begged him to let me and a couple of friends sleep in the tree house before the end of the summer. Finally he said yes, and we camped out in the tree, until I woke up about three in the morning to discover I was alone because everyone else had gone home. It wasn't an adventure without my friends, so I went in the back door of my house and fell asleep in my own bed.

"When I went back into my house my dad heard the door close, and he got up to see what was happening. That was when he looked out and saw our weirdo neighbor who lived with five dozen cats climbing up the ladder."

They were speechless. Mission accomplished.

"Dad, you never mentioned you had a tree house."

After two weeks of nonstop begging I built one. Safety was always an issue, so I used dinosaur-bone-size bolts to hook it to the tree so it would be able to withstand a category-three hurricane before I'd have to call my insurance adjuster, who would inform me that I could not file a claim for something that was illegally constructed in violation of every building code in my town's big book of dumb rules.

In a moment of absolute coincidence that shows that there is some sort of cosmic connection between fathers and their sons, during one of our final supply runs to Home Depot, my boy, Peter, noticed one particular option they were selling for tree forts that he wanted to install on his deluxe custom tree house. So I bought a sunshine yellow steering wheel.

I wanted to tell him that I had built my own steering wheel once, but he'd think I was about to launch into another one of those sepia-stained stories about walking five miles to school in the snow or writing with chalk on the back of a shovel, so I stopped and screwed the steering wheel to a beam next to the trapdoor.

"Every boy should have a tree house," I announced to my wife at its grand opening.

"It's too high." She had a point—it was. In fact, at that moment it was by far the most dangerous thing on our property.

I'd spent almost five hundred dollars on our backyard tower of terror, and after my wife's pronouncement of danger, our children were programmed to think that if they fell out, at the very least they'd spend the rest of their lives in an iron lung parked in the living room. On the plus side, we were the only ones on the block with a tree house that required an oxygen mask.

My son, for whom I built the high-altitude apartment, spent over the years a sum total of six minutes in the tree house, which averages out to about eighty-three dollars per minute of use. If I had it to do over again, I'd just give him a hundred-dollar bill and have him stand on my shoulders until the blood drained from my head and I wised up.

Tree houses, rafts, and fishing are charming things our parents did once upon a time but should now be verboten. I think it's time to cut the cord on obsolete outdoor activities. If it doesn't have an Underwriters Laboratories tag on it, don't use it. We simply aren't the same people we were two generations ago. Just ask a seventh-grade boy his impressions of Huckleberry Finn.

"Huckle*berry* . . . that's a new Tazo at Starbucks, right?"

This past weekend my wife, Kathy, and I were walking in our backyard and came to a stop under our long-abandoned tree house. "One of these days I should probably take that down." Initially dangerous, it was presently full of dangling tree branches, making it even more hazardous. It was sun baked and faded; the only piece still in good shape was the still bright yellow steering wheel on the side of the tree house.

"Maybe you could drive it into somebody else's tree," my wife said, smiling.

"At least it didn't sink," I said, flashing back to the Great Cow Pasture Disaster of 1967, another inglorious moment in our family history better left alone. We adjourned to the house, where my wife prepared a splendid meal of fried catfish that I had personally caught earlier that day at Safeway.

6

Jobs

I Was a Teenage Bread Pirate

exus makes mustard?" I marveled at the high-end selection of foods as I put the jar in my cart next to the Rolex tomato paste. This was the fantastic gourmet grocery store where I'd gotten my high school freshman son, Peter, a part-time job. It was a monument to food, with live lobsters over by the Kobe beef, down the aisle from the high-end imported meats and cheeses, and with every variety of fresh vegetable and fruit, and desserts fit for a state dinner. My boy was hired as a stock boy, but at this swanky place, we dubbed him a "stock analyst."

After his first eight-hour shift Peter reported that a high school chum saw him at work. "He said something like I didn't know your family was broke, putting the kids to work."

"What did you tell him?"

"That you work in cable."

In fact the job was Peter's idea because he wanted to make some money, and I wanted him to learn the value of a buck, so why not work at that store that sold monster shrimp for thirty-nine dollars a pound? Indeed, Peter learned the value of a dollar—that one buck could buy one-thirty-ninth of a pound of shrimp.

Two years later I persuaded my daughter Mary to apply for a job as a checkout girl at the same Gucci of groceries. On her first day, her first customer welcomed her to the world of work. "You are the dumbest person I have ever seen!" the shopper wailed at my honors-student daughter when she was unable to scan, bag, and provide change as fast as a Ginsu knife salesman hopped up on Red Bull and absinthe.

Later an infamous titan of industry yelped, "Don't you dare, missy," as Mary started to swipe his groceries through the checkout scanner. "The radiation from that will poison my food. Ring it up manually," said the freaky Fortune 500 CEO. How did this dingbat make it up the corporate ladder? Usually companies don't hire a person for the corner office when he arrives for the job interview wearing a three-piece suit and a tinfoil hat.

Meanwhile her own classmates who'd seen her behind the cash register dissed her with "Nice bow tie, Mary," a not-so-subtle reminder that she was somehow less of a person than they because she wore a uniform and they had the freedom to wear whatever slutty belly shirt they chose.

That town was a precious enclave of wealth, fame, and attitude, and while many were privileged, there was one customer who was always friendly and courteous and respectful of Mary as a person: a very famous rapper from Run-D.M.C.

He was the polar opposite of an alarmingly high number of customers who would say something mean or unkind. Every Sunday night when I'd pick her up after her shift she'd get into my car and break down in tears. We love the family that runs the place and I'd thought this would be a great job, but I had not factored in a few of the patrons who had her sweating like James Gandolfini on a StairMaster. So we pulled the plug.

Getting my kids a first job at a grocery store was what my father had done for me, when he talked a friend into hiring me in my hometown of Industry, Kansas. Misnamed because there was no actual industry in Industry; apparently the town founders had figured that if they named it that, America's industrialists who needed to plunk their smokestacks somewhere would flock to our town, which they did not. Industry was small, and sleepy, a cozy hometown that was much like TV's Mayberry, without the crack law-enforcement team.

My place of employment was a shiny silver-painted Depression-era storefront on the main drag. It was a simple emporium featuring miscellaneous canned foods, starchy snacks, and every imaginable bug-killing concoction. The back wall had a free-standing deli case packed with freshly ground hamburger and various "lunch meats": bologna; braunschweiger; and, from the *Who-Eats-This-Stuff?* category, headcheese, a vile amalgam of "head" parts harvested from the fatty noggins of barnyard animals that unwittingly volunteered for the job.

A small store required a small staff; we had a deli guy, a cashier, somebody to walk the bags out to the car for the old ladies, and a bookkeeper who'd balance the cash drawer at the end of the day. It was a four-person job, and I was all four of the people. I was also thirteen years old. Forget the child-labor laws designed to protect indentured children in overseas sweatshops from getting a dime a day to stitch soccer balls; I got a buck an hour, paid in cash at the end of the day, completely off the books because it was way south of the minimum wage.

There was one terrific fringe benefit: I could eat whatever I wanted. And the choice was always easy—this store featured Fanestil's, the filet mignon of boiled ham. For a kid who carried peanut butter and bologna on Wonder bread every day to school for lunch, Fanestil's ham tasted like a slice of hog heaven. Too pricey for my family to buy at a buck ninety-nine per pound, for the store's lone Saturday employee it was on the house. During my fifteen-minute orientation on how to operate the store, the owner suggested that I grab a bite during a slow time before or after lunch. "Just shave off two or three nice thick slices of whatever you like."

"Okay. Where's the bread?" I wondered.

Pointing toward the bread rack, the owner instructed, "Take any kind you like. My favorite's Roman Meal." And with that he pulled out a loaf of the rust-orange-wrapped bread, undid the twist tie, and stuck his hand in the bag. "I generally go about a quarter of the way back," he said, pulling out two pieces. "Don't ever take the heel, or whoever buys it is going to know that something's missing," he added as he rewrapped it and replaced it on the shelf.

My first day on the job and I was learning the dirty little secret of small-town America's grocery stores—bread embezzlement. Apparently the owner had learned this trick from another shopkeeper, who reasoned that it was wasteful to open up a whole loaf, because by the time the single employee got around to finishing off a whole loaf, it would be as stale as a *Hee Haw* rerun. So the boss officially authorized me to be a bread pirate. It was the only store in America I knew of where bread was sold "as is."

Later in high school I was lucky to get the best job in Clay Center, at a beautiful menswear store right on the courthouse square. The store's previous high school guy employee was graduating, and they needed a new kid who would invest every available nonschool hour there for two bucks an hour, which was double my grocery store loot. They also sent me to a menswear seminar in Kansas City where I sat in a room for an hour and was later given a certificate that said I was a *professional fashion consultant*. Years later my wife would ask me if things she was wearing matched.

"Well . . . as a professional fashion consultant . . ." and I'd launch into a theoretical discussion on aesthetics, making her wish she'd never asked me whether her stripes matched her plaids.

I was the only professional fashion consultant in my high school class. But there was a downside to being the youngest, limberest guy on the payroll—when Bob Finger, my boss, would point at a customer: "Steve, go size and fit that guy."

"Size and fit" was what we'd do with formal-wear-rental customers as they tried on different jackets to find their correct coat size. Then, to calculate their proper rental pants, I'd measure their waist, and then I'd get down on hands and knees, take a deep breath, and measure the inseam, which was from about an inch off the floor northbound to the area where their pants stopped and *they* started, a task that still haunts me twenty-five years later.

"Hey, getting a little personal down there, Nancy!" one farmer said, and I instantly took a pledge never to get that precise again. Who cared if his drawers were droopy? I was a salesman, not a proctologist.

When I graduated, the staff of Summers Menswear threw me a party at the town's country club and presented me with the best possible gift, luggage, which I would haul around from place to place, job to job, for the next twenty years. During my college years I needed to make a lot of money over the short summer, so my father asked one of his friends to hire me at union-scale wages as a plumber's assistant. Plumbing was a highly mechanical and technical trade, and seemed daunting for a guy whose last job was akin to giving strangers a prostate exam.

The job site was a future assisted-living home, where I would be the second man on a two-man crew to install a quarter of a mile of black cast-iron drainpipe in the foundation. My boss was a plumber named Dick Landers, who upon my arrival handed me my own set of blueprints, which I unrolled and stared at blankly. I must have looked like a monkey reading a map.

"You've got 'em sideways," my new boss told me, flipping them over and then giving me a general overview of what the blue lines meant. He knew I was clueless, but I was young and strong and he needed me to carry the cast-iron pipes. It was a collaboration of necessity, and barely into our first hour he revealed the absolute secret to plumbing.

"Here's all you need to know," he said in a low voice, so eavesdropping electricians nearby couldn't hear. With seven words he was able to sagely sum up gravity and capitalism. "Crap don't run uphill, and payday's Friday."

Over the next three months, with some days north of one hundred degrees, we finished the job. It was one of the most personally satisfying things I'd ever done. The two of us plumbed eighty-four units. Some days when my boss had an errand to run, I did the master plumbing myself. I'm sure that was against the rules, but who cares now? That was almost thirty years ago. When I'm back home I sometimes drive by that place, where I have not seen a sign saying "Elderly and infirmed forced to evacuate due to hideous plumbing malfunction," so I guess we did a good job.

I had a lot of manual-labor jobs, each uniquely challenging and requiring a different skill set. My father wanted me to learn to work with my hands, just as he had, giving me something to fall back on if my dream of becoming a world-famous cardiac surgeon didn't pan out.

My wife and I thought that aside from having regular after-school jobs, it was important that the kids help someone other than themselves. Peter worked at Camp Sunshine with the disabled, as did Mary, who in her senior year in high school took her sister Sally with her twice a week to read homework assignments to a pair of severely vision-impaired children.

Just like my father, I nudged my kids into getting jobs and seeing the real world with their own eyes. Of course times had changed; I never had to work a newfangled checkout scanner that poisoned fifty-dollar-a-pound Kobe beef. But my kids never learned how to pilfer Wonder bread two slices at a time. My now college-aged son, Peter, has graduated from the grocery and has since worked two summers at a prestigious law firm on Wall Street, where he spent more money on parking and the ferry than I made in two weeks at his age.

"Today this skinny contortionist bent over completely backward until he had his feet by his ears!" my son said, recalling a street performer he'd seen at the South Street Seaport. He told me the story as enthusiastically as he'd reported on the guy he saw on Comedy Central who had gas to the tune of the *William Tell* Overture.

"Then the contortionist, with his feet by his ears, walked over and put himself in a one-foot-by-one-foot glass box."

"Wow, did you tip him?"

"Dad, I'm saving for college," he said apologetically, "so I pretended I didn't speak English."

Trying to amass his fortune. One day he'll make the connection that just like him, that performer was trying to make a living. Eventually he'll drop a buck in his box, as long as the contortionist isn't in it. Personally, I would have given the guy a ten, because with him bent over backward, feet at his face, measuring his inseam would have been a snap.

I'm proud of the fact that my kids got a head start on their peers in the world of work, and one day when they're a bit older I will reveal to them the final piece to the employment puzzle they'll need to know to survive the real world of work. It's something I've applied to every job I've had since I wore a hard hat.

"Kids, listen up. . . . Crap don't run uphill, and payday's Friday."

My children will then sit there for a moment to contemplate the hugeness of this thought and how they could apply it to their own situations. Then my youngest daughter will bolt from her seat and scream toward the kitchen, "Mommy! Daddy said 'crap'!"

7

Dexterous Dad

My Father Is Martha Stewart

Every year my friend Rich Collier won the science fair, but he had help from his father. His dad, Chet, was a television executive who would personally order the carpenters at *The Mike Douglas Show* to build whatever Rich wanted, and they did. Who knows? I might have gotten a science scholarship if only my father had run *The Tonight Show Starring Johnny Carson*.

Fathers are the default parent when a school project involves elbow grease, duct tape, or power tools that could result in the loss of a pinkie. But I didn't want to be the typical dad, and when my son Peter was in grade school, I wanted him to do the work himself unless he needed help. A second-grade assignment arrived at home to "diagram the atom," and he immediately waved me away. Instantly proud of my four-foot Bob Vila, I didn't see his final product until back-to-school night. His mother and I reveled in the way our son cleverly depicted the atom's orbit with licorice whips and how the neutrons, protons, and electrons were dramatized by gumdrops and jellybeans. It wasn't so much a science project as a vending-machine explosion.

Hoping to catch some other parent's envious glances at my boy's handiwork, I let my eyes drift down the display to compare my son's work with his classmates'. One seven-year-old had a model of the atom's orbit built from construction-grade copper pipe. It cleverly used a toilet float ball as the nucleus. The copper alone would have cost over a hundred dollars, before labor and parts and attitude. The boy who built it was coincidentally the son of a plumber.

A girl named Tiffany used five tandem Lite Brites to depict the Hertzsprung-Russell diagram, which shows the temperature of the stars. Her dad was a government astronomer for NASA.

Then it occurred to me: the kids in Peter's class didn't do this work, their fathers did, and that was cheating! The dirty little secret of grade school is that every day of every week, homework arrives, and fathers adjourn to the garage to build their child a good grade. A bit rattled by my son's project, which looked so . . . childlike, I pledged, "Next time I'm helping him . . . whether he wants help or not."

A lot was on the line. If I didn't help him with the projects now, he wouldn't get into a good school or get a good job, so he couldn't help me out later in life, which would mean that penniless and deep in my eighties, I'd have to open a roadside souvenir shop where, curiously, I'd develop the accent of a Louisiana catfish wrestler.

"Build the solar system" was his next homework project. I immediately started planning. "How do you want to do it?" I asked Peter as he excitedly briefed me on his master plan to use flimsy construction paper as the background and depict the planets with ballpoint pen and ho-hum crayon illustration. He was describing a well-intentioned piece of scientific garbage that was a one-way ticket to a career collecting tolls on the Garden State Parkway.

"Hey, buster, I told you last time, we don't take Hardee's coupons!"

"Peter, that's a *very* good idea," I said, "but how about if we do it this way . . ." and off I launched into my plan B, which would involve X-Acto knives, actual electricity, three trips to the hobby store, and enough airplane glue to sedate Jimi Hendrix.

"What if they find out you did it?" my little innocent boy asked.

"Peter, it's still your project. I'm only helping." And with that I dismissed him so that I could concentrate on his handiwork. I'd inherited the do-it-yourself spirit from my father, who during my 4-H years would design and build various projects for the county fair that would win purple ribbons and a trip to the state fair, so I credit my father for giving me the "crafty gene."

"Dad, that's sweet," Peter said when he first laid eyes on his finished project.

Styrofoam balls were scaled in size to the planets: Jupiter big foam ball, Venus little ball, Neptune mediumish. The planets were correctly airbrushed and then suspended with black wire hangers that kept them hovering a few inches above a huge three-by-six-foot piece of museum-quality black foam core. To add drama, I'd taken two strings of miniature Christmas lights and poked the heads through the foam to depict the Milky Way. It was stunning and the only science project that year that had a huge carbon footprint, which back then was what I thought you left after walking through a Boy Scout campfire.

Peter dragged it through the door of his classroom, and his teacher exclaimed, "Oh, that's wonderful!" Three days later the grade arrived home, and happily I got an A+. Did I say "I got"? I meant *he got* an A+. I just supervised a bit, if anybody's asking, but may I remind you we're not under oath here?

Such a dramatically large and scientifically accurate representation, Peter's solar-system project was permanently displayed in the library. A year later when a well-intentioned janitor tried to dust it, he accidentally knocked off Pluto, sending it rolling off to a fate unknown. The planet's disappearance led some of the more uncouth children who apparently had planet confusion to remark to my son, "Hey, Peter, what happened to *Uranus*?"

That solar system would remain on display for years as a testament to the fine work the students at this school were churning out on a daily basis. HA! Teachers know exactly who does the big projects. If one day a kid turns in an assignment with pipe cleaners and Popsicle sticks, chances are he got help from his parents when the next week he drags in an actual working heart bypass machine.

"Brandon, where did you get the idea to build that?" his teacher might inquire. An immediate and awkward silence is followed quickly by "Upon advice of counsel I shall not answer that question on the grounds that it would violate my Fifth Amendment rights." Not only is his dad a doctor, but his mother is a lawyer, and they have a joint subscription to *Martha Stewart Living*.

Maybe with my first child I overdid it. I would not make that mistake with Mary. When she brought home a social studies assignment with a selection of projects, she had the choice of constructing a wigwam, Conestoga wagons, a tribal headdress, or one of several lanyard-based knotting items. We selected the absolute hardest project possible, a scale model of a Viking ship. Three days and four trips to Home Depot, and the fleet of one was done.

"Mary . . . come look," I announced with the tone of a proud father who'd just given birth to a 737-toothpick ship.

She'd assumed that like her older brother her only involvement in her school project would be dragging it from the car to the classroom, but I wanted her to actually do something, so I explained that she would have to paint it. I'd laid out the brushes and a smock, and opened a window for proper ventilation. How hard could that be? With my apprentice now in charge, I adjourned to the kitchen for a cup of coffee and then read the paper to see what I'd missed over the long weekend while I was in dry dock.

Returning to marvel at her progress, I was expecting to see her use the horsehair hobby brush with small strokes, carefully applying paint with the light touch of an impressionist. Instead I witnessed her pouring a river of paint directly out of the can and letting it pool on the deck of the ship.

"WHAT ARE YOU DOING?" I yelled in capitals.

"It's how they paint M&Ms."

But we weren't building M&Ms, we were in the shipbuilding business, and now the ship I'd spent my entire week's allotment of naptime on was a gooey gloppy mess. I caught myself yelling a little and had to remind myself that it was her project, not mine, and rather than say another cross word I'd have shot staples under my fingernails.

"Daddy, I'm sorry."

"No worries, it looks great," I said as I flipped the ship over and drained a pint of paint. Once dry you could not tell it had once been through a Benjamin Moore hurricane. To christen it she wanted to use the Swedish version of her name. Sitting at the family computer in the kitchen with her mother, Mary Googled "Swedish name for Mary." Within one second there were over thirty-nine thousand hits, and most of these Swedish Marys were pictured naked, interacting with men who doubtless answered to Sven, for three dollars and ninety-five cents a minute. Without mentioning what she'd seen she made a spontaneous change.

"Let's call it the *St. Lucia*," which she hand-lettered on the bow. It was fine with me because I love Lucy. She got an A on the project.

At the end of the line of my parental duties with my third and final child I came to the realization, as all fathers eventually do, that while my two eldest children got great grades, they might not have learned much from their projects, because their type A father had done all the work. Last chance I would take on the role simply of a creative consultant: if something needed to be cut with a saw or other power tool, I'd happily do that; otherwise, throughout her entire grade-school career she did it all.

On Sally's back-to-school night we beheld the projects by Sally's class. Several looked like they'd been purchased outright on the Internet; one was quite possibly produced by Industrial Light and Magic. Amid the smoke and mirrors was Sally's, a replica of the *Discovery* space shuttle. She had done all the work and it looked like it. Posted at the bottom was her grade: A+.

Sometimes it takes raising a couple of kids before a father figures out how to do it right. With our first two, I did the hard work; with my last girl, she did it herself, and today she is the handiest of my children. Every trip to Lowe's or Home Depot, she'd ride shotgun, and anytime the mom needed a small home repair or something restored to its original position, Sally would do it. And here's the proud part: she learned how to do all of that stuff by watching me, just as I learned watching my dad.

Every teacher in America can spot a father's fingerprints on his children's work, and I think the reason they don't bust us is because they know in the long run it's good to have kids and parents collaborate. On our final back-to-school night, I pulled aside my youngest daughter's teacher and asked how she was doing.

"Nobody tries harder, and nobody is sweeter than Sally." It was the kind of report every parent dreams of hearing.

A moment later a school administrator wandered by to chat, and I pointed to my son's legendary solar system still on display.

"It has withstood the test of time," they said, beaming, even though we both knew they'd been passing my work off as that of a typical fourth-grade student for years.

Pointing to the missing planet, I asked, "By the way, did they ever find Uranus?"

There was an immediate eruption of laughs from the other nearby fathers. The administrator, showing he could not only take a joke but give one, handed me an official detention slip that indicated I was to report after the event to the cafeteria. As a local taxpayer who needed his beauty sleep, I certainly did not.

However, had I gone I could have chatted with other detained parents, taking great satisfaction in knowing that while we were all a little older and grayer, we could still do grade A work on the fifth-grade level.

8

Rivalry

Never Lick a Steak Knife

Thanks to my wife's three pregnancies and several knee operations I discovered there are a trio of machines a man filling in for his bride should never attempt to operate: a washer-dryer, a kitchen stove, and, for painfully obvious reasons, a breast pump. Just seeing a guy try to find the on switch for the last item would be as hilarious as watching Richard Simmons wander the tool corral at Home Depot.

"Honey, remember, all of the world's greatest chefs are men," I announced shortly after my wife deputized me as chief food-preparation officer. Still recuperating from a knee surgery, she was splayed out watching *Oprah* as I slid open the deck door to preheat the only cooking contraption a man is truly comfortable operating, my 75,000 BTU natural-gas and semiatomic grill. It was the closest thing on our homestead to a vulcanizing killing machine.

"Mommy! Daddy's baking brownies in the barbecue!" my youngest proudly announced to my wife, who was surely trying to recall the phone number for the pizza place that was on standby to provide our family with sustenance whenever I destroyed entire meals. I had never heard of anyone baking brownies on the grill, but it seemed possible; besides, there was the possibility I was on the verge of a culinary showstopper that family members would talk about for years to come.

"They're perfect!" I announced thirty-two minutes after I stuck the brownies into the grill, waving them under the nose of my wife, who seemed pleasantly surprised. I tried not to gloat in the direction of my wife, because she had never made molten brownie surprise before. Once they were cool to the touch, I started to cut up the pan of brownies, but a funny thing happened on the way to dessert—I pushed and I plunged, yet I couldn't jam the knife any deeper than a half inch. Suddenly the hint of a smile appeared on my wife's face; maybe the perfect meal wasn't so perfect after all.

"Dad, what's the matter with the brownies?"

Apparently Duncan Hines's technicians had concocted their recipe for preparation with actual kitchen appliances, not a roaring unbridled gas grill. To the naked eye it looked like a brownie, but the bottom half had undergone some chemical reaction and had fused itself together as an impenetrable brown briquette.

"Sally, go get me the *widow maker*."

She knew exactly what I wanted, a knife that was a gift from a hunter friend and had arrived in a box that said it was suitable for gutting a moose, puncturing the tire of an approaching enemy troop carrier, or cutting your arm off if stuck on a mountainside. My immediate plan was simple: I would cut the brownies into squares and then slice the tasty brownie top from its concrete-basement bottom layer.

The widow maker made quick work of my cooking calamity. I was able to easily cut up about a dozen two-inch brownie squares. "By cooking everything on one grill we didn't dirty as many pans, didn't heat up the house, and saved some time and plenty of electricity." I made a note to myself never to utter any of that aloud again, as I felt I sounded like Paula Deen and Al Gore's love child.

With the brownie squares, I would next cut the top layer from the rock-hard bottom, fillet style. Initially I applied a lot of pressure cutting through what felt like iron until I suddenly hit a soft spot, which, given the pressure I was using, sent the knife careening haphazardly through the rest of the brownie, quickly exiting and coming to a stop in midair only after slashing across the top of my middle finger, cleanly lopping off the tip. With the end of my finger then hanging by a thread as I looked at it for a moment, I thought, That has got to hurt.

Within two seconds the hysterical department of my brain received the message from my hand. Our backyard had not witnessed such a melee since a bat swooped out of the sky, knocked himself out cold on the lemonade pitcher, and fell into a bowl of coleslaw, prompting my entire family to bolt from the table as if they had electrodes wired directly to their tonsils.

"Daddddddyyyyyyy!" Sally screamed. *"I'll get the ice!"*

The only ice that I needed at that moment was Smirnoff Ice, a really tall one, applied directly to my finger as an antiseptic and then directly into my bloodstream because I *JUST CUT OFF MY FIN-GERTIP!*

With blood squirting out *Monty Python* style, my wife, always cool under pressure, took charge. "You need a stitch," she announced as she grabbed her crutches, ready to drive me immediately to the I-told-you-so entrance of our local hospital. Because the fingertip was hanging by a thread, the do-it-yourselfer in me flapped it back in place, and I then applied pressure and pigheadedness to stop the bleeding. There was another reason I didn't want to go: The last time I went to the ER was the day I dropped a four-by-eight sheet of plywood with a razor-sharp edge on my big toenail, which split into a disgusting stump of toe and blood, prompting the doctor to observe, "Oh my God, I'm not touching that!" and he did not. But he did charge me $145 for the privilege of scaring him.

Back to the current self-mutilation. I fully bandaged and Neosporined my finger and then defiantly returned to the table, which was a culinary crime scene with blood spatters everywhere; the only thing missing was a little chalk outline around the brownie pan. With my middle finger bandaged thickly I kept it raised above heart level, making me look like I was flipping off somebody while making a pledge: "Do you promise never to do anything really incredibly stupid or dangerous in the kitchen, so help you God?"

"I do. Will somebody get Daddy the barrel of Advil from Costco?"

Everybody seemed happy that their sugar daddy would survive the night, and a little surprised that the first thing I did after dodging the loss of an extremity was return to my chore and cut the edible brownie from its mortar bottom.

"Dad, you can't make us eat them," my son, Peter, our in-house garbage can, said, surprising me. Unable to convince a single one of my children and certainly not my wife, I dined alone on what was the most painful dessert I'd ever created.

My wife makes the best meals imaginable, always healthy and creative. I don't know whatever possessed me to think I could compete with her in her arena. If I'm ever called upon again to substitute for my wife in the kitchen, we're going to a restaurant, we'll get takeout, or as a last resort I'll get a family-sized IV drip bag full of glucose (which is very filling) from one of my friends in surgical scrubs.

Fathers are great at many things, but they can never replace a mother, so don't even bother trying. I'm lousy in the kitchen and barely better in the laundry. While saving money on dry cleaning I found it an absolute breeze to shrink two of my wife's new Lilly Pulitzer skirts to the size of a pair of tube socks. She was furious until my daughter realized that the newly remodeled skirts would handily fit an overlooked member of the family, Malibu Barbie.

9

Sports

The Coach Bag

When of kindergarten age, our son, Peter, started his sports career. We arrived at his first practice on a chilly October morning afraid he was more likely to catch a cold than a pass. We layered him first with long johns, then a polar fleece sweat suit, and over it all his actual jersey and shorts. In these thermal yet restrictive clothing choices, he had the on-field mobility of the Tin Man in *The Wizard of Oz*.

The soccer field was next to an abandoned Nike missile silo that once stood vigil for nearby Washington, D.C., and although the Cold War was wrapping up, in the back of our heads we always worried that some rogue Russian general might push the button and take out a league of Kinder Kickers.

From a father's perspective sports are great because they help a child develop athletic and social skills as their parents hang out and gossip about the neighbors who sleep around. We became friendly with every parent except one father. Brendan was a good boy and great player, but I avoided his dad, who was then the director of the FBI, Louis Freeh. Rumor had it the Mafia, small-time crooks from up the river, and some little-known group of radical Islamic extremists with a name that had a bunch of vowels in it all wanted him dead. And standing on the sideline drinking a Dunkin' Donut hazelnut coffee made him a sitting duck. Why should I stand next to him?

Don't get me wrong, I'm a big athletic supporter, but I had to draw the line at political assassination.

In our town there was a fair and balanced rule that every child must play half of every game, but a number of my son's coaches, who shall remain nameless for the purpose of avoiding lawsuits, refused. They would put him in with thirty seconds left in the first half and then in the second half for the last one minute if the team was winning.

"What are you talking about? He played both halves, didn't he?" one of his coaches would say. "Okay, maybe I made a mistake, but next time he'll start. See you Saturday." He never started on Saturday.

Warming the bench in baseball, Peter was called to pinch-hit for one of the starters, who'd gotten hurt. Peter strode to the plate exactly as two hometown celebrities arrived at the game.

"Hey, it's Phil Simms!" somebody yelled, and the entire bench and every head of every parent in the stands turned around to get a good look at two-time Super Bowl quarterback Phil Simms and his son Chris. During that moment of stargazing, the only two people at the game paying attention were my son and the pitcher, who threw his first pitch low and outside. Peter was used to not playing in a game, so despite a bad pitch he took a step toward the ball and whacked it good. The crack of the bat surprised both teams, who stopped looking at the Simmses and tried to find the ball. They had no idea where it was.

"Take three!" the third-base coach yelled, but Peter knew Phil Simms was watching and would later apologize for running past third and heading for home.

"Peter, *go back to third!*" his coach was yelling, and for good reason—the ball was now in the glove of our town's best player. Within three seconds Peter would be toast.

"Slide, Peter, slide!" my wife yelled in that "Run, Forrest, run" voice.

A cloud of dust and a moment of hesitation as the ball and the boy arrived at home plate simultaneously.

"He's safe!"

The entire crowd went wild because nobody had ever seen him play before, let alone get his first home run.

"Good hit, kid," Phil Simms said when he passed Peter on the way out. I entertained the idea of hiring the Super Bowl legend for all of the team's home games, but his asking price was too much, and the only player I could afford, Mookie Wilson, did not have the same impact on the team's psyche.

Despite his first home run and a sensational slide home, coaches thought it was a fluke, and Peter spent much of the next three seasons on the bench. By seventh grade, out of twenty-one sports and twenty-one coaches, Peter had had two who always put him in, Jim Madormo and Rob Gephardt. Most of the rest usually had an excuse for why their sons played the whole game and Peter warmed the bench. With a single season left before high school ball, I knew that unless Peter played a lot, he'd never make it to the varsity team, which was his dream. After seven seasons of humiliation there was just one thing to do.

I volunteered to coach.

If *SportsCenter* had my highlight reel it would consist of a single inopportune football mix-up where I surprisingly scored for the other team. At the end of that game I was informed by the basketball coach that during the upcoming basketball season, I would be going out for wrestling.

My wife is the complete volunteer at our house, a Sunday school teacher, Scout leader, Academic Decathlon sponsor, team booster, and room mother. I'm envious because she can do anything; I, on the other hand, am best suited to be an organ donor.

Unquestionably unqualified to coach, I picked up *Coaching for Dummies,* a whistle, a clipboard, and a can of Cruex. I never needed that but was flattered if people thought I might be so sweaty that I would. Now that I had the gear, all I needed was a bunch of boys. At the town baseball draft, one father-coach had an Excel spreadsheet with the record of everybody going back to third grade; another had a chart with cut-and-paste faces of each kid in our town. For my preparation Peter wrote down the names of the kids he wanted on the team on the back of a Visa bill envelope.

An elaborate formula, based upon how each coach's son had been rated the previous season, would determine who'd get the first pick. The other fathers had all coached before and each gave his kid the highest mark, the local equivalent of giving your son a Heisman. Peter's previous coach never put him in, so he was given the lowest score, which meant I got the first pick. I selected the best player in town and checked off one name on the Visa bill.

Over the next excruciating hour tempers flared, feelings were hurt, and lies were told. On my second pick one of the fathers told me why I couldn't get the best pitcher in town: "He's a family friend and I promised his dad I'd drive his son to practice." I let the guy take the kid, and later asked the father of the pitcher.

"Who? I've never met that guy."

Liar, liar, clipboard on fire.

No wonder they wouldn't put Peter in. Some of these guys would stop at nothing to win. Much to their horror I wound up with all but one of the names on the Visa bill, and we wound up with a roster so powerful that they still refer to it in our town as the Illegal Rec Team of 2001. There was one problem: me. So I turned to Peter, who'd studied the game from the bench; he would make up each game's lineup. During practices and games when I was clueless I'd quietly ask our catcher, Michael, the son of a great coach, for some guidance.

"Michael?" I'd practically whisper.

"What, Mr. Doocy?"

"Was that a strike?"

"No, it was low and outside."

"Ball, low and outside!" I'd announce in a clear strong voice, reassuring the parents in the stands that I knew what I was doing.

Of all of the things I've done with my son, that season was our best time together. Not only was it great, but it had a *Movie of the Week* ending—the clueless coach's team wound up in the town's World Series. It came down to the final inning, and when I told the son of another coach that he was going to pitch, but he informed me that his dad wouldn't let him, I had to turn to somebody who'd pitched only one game before, our catcher, Michael. With the score tied and the title on the line, he seemed to be struggling, so I called the first time-out of my career and took the long walk to the mound.

"When the coach comes out here to the mound, what is he supposed to tell the pitcher, Michael?"

"To throw strikes, Coach."

"Didn't you already know that?"

"Yes, sir."

"Okay, I think we're done."

A triumphant season—we took second place. My mission was accomplished: Peter got the experience he needed and would play four years of high school baseball, exactly why I had volunteered. That night at my retirement dinner my daughter Mary surprised me. "I thought you were going to be my coach!"

Quid pro coach.

Coaching middle-school girls was like herding cats. They didn't pay attention, and desperately trying to focus them, I found myself screaming instructions. By the third week I was waking up with the husky voice of Brenda Vaccaro.

The throat doctor told me, "You've got a bad case of preacher's notch," a syndrome named after hellfire and brimstone ministers who preached to the flock at high volume. "Don't feel bad. A lot of guys get this. You a stock trader?"

"Girls' coach."

Understanding the torture, he prescribed two weeks of no talking. Apparently the doctor was a CNN viewer and didn't know what I did. At work I continued to speak, about half as loudly as usual, but

at practices and games I did a lot of pointing and pantomime. One
of my most innovative ideas was when we were behind, I'd get a buck
out of my wallet and wave it.

"Dollar offense!" one of my players would holler.

The other team would be impressed that we had names for plays,
when in fact "dollar offense" simply meant whoever scored would get
a dollar from me. It was very effective; I'm sure other coaches would
be horrified, but I'm confident that by now the statute of limitations
has run out on my playola.

Once again my team was in the playoffs. My daughter Mary, our
best pitcher, was on the mound when the opposing father-coach
opened his yap trap. "Girls, don't worry, this pitcher can't get it across
the plate. She's terrible!" No wonder that nitwit had made his own
daughter cry one inning earlier. "Is that the best you can do, honey?"
he asked my daughter, who was now crying on the mound. Her sister, Sally, led the bench in a chant: "Mary, Mary, she's our woman, if
she can't do it nobody can!"

"Hey, shorty," the evil coach said in the direction of my youngest.
"Put down the pom-poms."

I had heard enough and was ready to give him a reason to get that
much-deserved nose job. I stared him down as I walked out to the
pitching circle, where I told my daughter that if she didn't finish the
inning, the terrorist would win.

Showing great poise, she retired the side to finish the inning, and
we won. But Coach Bigmouth had wrecked it for her forever—it was
the last time she'd ever pitch a ball. The next day I saw that guy in
church, where, I know, it was wrong for me to hope that a lightning
bolt would kill him on the spot, but sometimes a guy's mind wanders
during the sermon when they're asking for money.

Telling Mary I understood why she quit, I said I would too, prompting my third grader Sally to wonder, "Did you forget about me? Now
you're my coach, right?"

Coaching little girls Sally's age was certainly the most fun because
they didn't care about the score, or accuracy; they were there mainly

for the snacks. One game there was so much giggling and inattention that I believe we fell behind during the national anthem.

Sally didn't really like to play, hated practice, and never came close to catching a ball. But it all changed the day my TV producer, Matt Singerman, called and asked, "Can one of your kids come in tomorrow? Cal Ripken has a book out about teaching kids to play ball, and he wants somebody to throw the ball to."

My older children were both busy that next day, leaving the girl who could not catch.

"Cal who?" When I told her, Sally then wondered, "Do I get a costume?"

"No uniform, but you'll be on television."

A television appearance was a great motivator. That night we practiced for hours, and the next day Cal Ripken threw a dozen balls her direction and she caught every one. The next day a couple of the cool kids told Sally they'd seen her on television, and she suddenly liked the game. She got better, more confident, and then she sandbagged me with the five scariest words for a father-coach.

"Dad, I want to pitch."

I wasn't worried about her losing the game—I could do that on my own. I worried about the heartless parents who would heckle her. So I made her a deal: "Let's practice, and if you're ready, you can pitch in the last game of the season."

I knew she'd forget about that the same way she'd forgotten her promises to walk the dog, water the garden, and feed the hermit crab. Remarkably, every day after school she practiced, and she got quite good. Peter helped, and we'd all drill in the backyard together. One day I promised to take them both to the Dairy Queen when we were done.

"Peter, one more pop-up," I said, trying to help my junior varsity third baseman with his fielding.

My last throw of the day was always the same pitch, a sky hook that I started down low behind my back and catapulted straight up about fifty feet. Exactly as I started to unwind with all the power

I could muster, Sally walked up behind me to ask if it was time to get ice cream. I didn't know she was there until the ball in my hand crashed into her eye.

"Go get Mommy!"

I could not breathe on the way to the hospital. Sally was screaming, my wife was crying, and I could plainly see the stitches from the ball on the cheekbone of this girl who had a visual disability and had already had an operation on that eye.

"Tell me she's not going to lose her eye," my wife pleaded with the emergency-room doctor.

"Let's see what the CAT scan shows."

"I'm so sorry, Sally," I repeated over and over as she lay motionless on the gurney, with a huge white ice pack covering her face. After the last of the tests, she started a breathy whisper: "Daddy?"

"Yes, pumpkin."

"Can I still pitch?"

"We'll see."

The doctor reappeared clutching some supersized X-rays. It was good news. Her glasses had somehow absorbed much of the initial force and distributed the impact; she'd escaped without a cracked skull and with just a bloody swollen eye, he explained as he put on an eye patch.

"She's one lucky girl."

Heading home from the emergency room, I insisted we detour to the Dairy Queen. This one time only, I was willing to spring for any menu item regardless of price. Banana Split, Peanut Butter Parfait, you name it. I was trying to buy my way out from under a ton of guilt. She asked for a green Mister Misty, a refreshing and economical selection.

Her elementary-school chums, especially the boys, marveled at her black eye for weeks. We told her to say, "You should see the other guy."

One week later she was out of her eye patch and standing in the pitcher's circle. It was the last inning of the last game, just as I'd promised. She'd practiced with her eye patched, but her depth perception was way off and she'd gotten only half of her pitches across the plate.

"Sally, hold it," I said, marching out to the circle for the second time in my coaching career. Putting a hand on each shoulder, I repeated the advice my catcher had given me years earlier in our town World Series.

"Throw strikes."

"I will, Daddy."

And then, like a maestro conducting his last orchestra, I raised my voice to the infield and said, "Ladies . . . in the immortal words of Robert Frost . . . let's kick some butt."

A howl went up, and it was game on. At the beginning of the season Sally could not catch the ball, and now, amazingly, she was our closing reliever. She threw the ball slowly and steadily, but mainly slowly. Between pitches she'd methodically find a good spot on the rubber, adjust her hair, then her hat, and then grip the ball exactly how she wanted it. Her routine was taking an excruciatingly long time. After about twenty minutes, with only one out, I could hear a parent complaining, "Brianna's going to miss her birthday party at one."

At the same time the teams for the next game were already there waiting to take the field, but they couldn't, because Sally was still pitching. I looked back at the stands to see some parents were giving me the take-her-out, let's-get-this-over-with look. But I was the coach, and this was why I had volunteered. I had invested 150 thankless hours over three months in their children; the least they could do was wait for mine.

The longest inning of my life was fifty-six minutes.

"Strike three, batter out!"

A cheer went up, and I walked out and picked her up. Coming in at the absolute end of the season and then successfully retiring the side, Sally was our family's version of Rudy.

"Can I pitch next year?" she asked.

"Why not?"

Sally decided that winter that she was done with sports, and spent more time at competitive dance, although she would eventually join the swim team, where as a freshman she swam on the varsity team that went to the state finals. I would never wear the coach T-shirt again, which freed up a lot of my time, yet it was surprisingly sad. I would miss the kids presenting me a coach gift at the end of the season like an oversized autographed ball with all of their names and a gift certificate to a restaurant that served hard liquor. But more than that I'd miss the time goofing around with my kids, doing things with them that would be our secrets from Mom, like the time my son entertained the bench by taking out his cup and using it as an oxygen mask (try explaining to the doctor why he had a case of jock itch on his sideburns).

It all ended that June afternoon after Sally's triumphant pitching debut. I was throwing the bat bag in the back of my car when a parent who was parked next to us said, "So, Coach, you finished in *fifth* place. How's it feel?"

That was easy.

"It feels . . . like *first.*"

10

Work

Take Mom's Spy to Work Day

Each year an estimated 20 million children tag along with their parents, who spend a full day pretending they have lots to do when in reality if the kid weren't there they'd spend slabs of free time sucking down coffee over by the copier with their office spouse or minimizing solitaire whenever a supervisor walked into their pod.

"Why's your home page Overstock.com, Daddy?"

A longtime supporter of this day of exploration, I always felt bad for children whose parents had unconventional jobs. What if their mother was a "lady of the evening"? What would their Take Your Child to Work Day be like?

"Kids, say hello to Mommy's boss, Slickback."

"Hi, Mr. Slickback. You have a nice Cadillac!"

Just like Mr. Slickback, I have an unconventional job. I don't work regular hours or in a regular office. I sit on a television sound stage for hours at a time as I pray that the high definition isn't revealing that I cut myself that morning, causing a single drop of blood to park itself on the collar of my wrinkle-free Brooks Brothers dress shirt. Cronkite never had to worry about HD; he could sit on camera with half a gallon of gravy on his tie and nobody noticed.

My children have all begged me to take them to work even though my wake-up time is 3:27 A.M. I know many other parents who also get up at 3:27 A.M., but that is just to pee.

My kids go because they never know when one of their idols will wind up on our show. During fourth grade my daughter Mary made the trip into New York City to interview Britney Spears, back when Mary and Britney were both still wearing underpants.

Peter was in high school when he demanded to go the day movie star Carmen Electra arrived, and although I'm not sure exactly how it happened, before she left, she'd promised Peter that she'd be his date for the junior prom. Watching *Entertainment Tonight* a month before the big date, we discovered that Carmen had gone off and married one of her many part-time husbands. Peter then made an emergency plan B to secure a mere mortal high school girl for a date, because we had at that time a crazy house rule that your prom date could not be married.

"But, Dad," he begged for a dispensation. "So what if she's married? It's Carmen Electra."

On the verge of saying, "Okay, but just this one time," I glanced over at my wife, who was giving me *the look*. I'd seen it before, in particular after an interview with actress Linda Evans. That morning my wife and children were at home watching me chat live on network television with Miss Evans about her *Dynasty* days and whatever product she was promoting. My wife noticed something unspoken, and shared: "Kids, I think Linda Evans is flirting with your father!"

In fact she was not flirting with me, she was simply being friendly, and I was in return simply trying to be a good host and to make her feel comfortable, so I'd laugh hysterically at everything she said.

"Wait a minute," my wife announced to our stunned children. "Your father is flirting with her!"

No child should have to hear that over cold cereal. They watched the rest of the interview in slack-jawed silence. When the segment was done and a commercial started, suddenly my wife and children had no idea of the immediate whereabouts of Linda Evans or me.

"Are you getting a divorce?" Mary, the middle child, inquired. My wife didn't answer. Six-year-old Sally burst into tears as she wondered if she'd just witnessed the final moments of our family thanks to some small talk with Krystle Carrington.

"Kids, say hello to your new mommy."

Mary joined Sally's crying jag. A lot of their friends had parents who split up, but it was usually over the landscaper, and certainly was never televised.

"Mommy," Peter wondered, "do you think Linda Evans has a swimming pool?"

Both girls stopped crying; Sally looked up midsniffle. "Do you think she does?"

Mary, whose television in her room was always tuned to *E! News Daily,* was also suddenly interested in a potential Hollywood branch to the family tree; she immediately saw a connection to a famous romance-novel hunk turned fake-butter salesman. "Mommy, would that make Fabio my stepfather?"

"You mean Yanni, and the answer is no. Show's over. We're going to school."

"Do you think Linda Evans would drive us to school?" Peter asked as the SUV door slammed the end to that conversation.

My wife learned the hard way that children are starstruck, especially when a celebrity may be coming to live at your house. And with my job I've sat down for many a thorough three-minute discussion with an endless trail of A-, B-, C-, and D-list stars selling their books, movies, TV shows, and other stuff, including ointments about which I never had the heart to ask where they were applied. Many former celebrities who've been away from the spotlight for a while leverage their fame on behalf of pharmaceutical companies making things like bladder control remedies and incontinence cures, and those guests we interview on a special plastic couch, for obvious reasons.

Our youngest, Sally, who went to work with me this past year, has never been that interested in the stars or glamour; she had a simple reason for wanting to go: "You let me have a Coke at four A.M."

There is a little-talked-about dark side to Take Your Child to Work Day: your kids are exposed to your coworkers. This is an actual transcript of a conversation I had with a colleague about my son.

"He's six five. How tall is your wife?"

"Five eight."

"You're only about six one," my office pal says. "How tall is the milkman?"

As a father four inches shorter than his twenty-one-year-old son, I can't tell you how many times I've heard that line of questioning. This inquisitor I would later freeze out at the coffeepot. My wife is a saint, and insinuating that my missus had slept with the milkman *was way over the line*. She has done many things over the years, but she has never been an easy broad who'd disrobe for dairy products.

Now T-bones or snow tires, that's another matter.

I must sign off for now—Linda Evans may be calling me on the phone upstairs.

11

Male Call

Things Only a Dad Can Teach a Boy

There are three things that a boy best learns from his father:
1. How to pee standing up
2. How to tie a tie without hanging himself
3. How to shave his face without losing a nostril

Before our son, Peter, was born we'd purchased everything we'd need for his first years of life, including a baby potty with twin giraffes, one on each side of the pot, which acted as handles that the child would grab to steady himself as he turned to sit down to do his business. We parked the giraffes right next to the real man-sized toilet in our downstairs bathroom.

One day when I was alone in the giraffe room washing my face, my almost two-year-old son wandered in, dropped trou, and stood there bare bottomed, waiting. This could be a baby-book moment, the first time he'd stand and deliver.

Thirty seconds went by but nothing happened. He was clearly wondering how to prime the pump when he mentally opened the floodgates and peed directly on the newly installed Laura Ashley wallpaper, completely missing the giraffes.

After Peter become the boy wizard I thought my job as the official standing-up-to-potty instructor was complete, but I was wrong. Two years later, three-year-old Mary, who was told she could not attend a preschool until she was potty trained, announced she was thirty seconds away from being toilet trained.

"Come here!"

Opening the door, I saw her standing over the giraffe toilet, then in its third year of service, her pants at the ankles. She smiled as she screwed up her face like she was squeezing something out, but nothing happened. We waited. And waited some more. Then she remembered a small detail about how her brother did it, and she grabbed her belly button, and within seconds she was standing there soaking her shoes.

"Good job, Mary," my wife enthused, relieved that she hadn't hit the yellowed wallpaper. Toilet training was easier than necktie tying.

"Over, under, around, and through" is something that I've shown my son dozens of times, and despite being an honors student at one of America's best universities, he can't do it. I'm still tying his ties. Before he leaves for a semester I'll knot up half a dozen of my favorites that he'll wear for a season and then return with various gravy and salsa spots.

My final dad-only chore was the most dangerous because when it came to teaching him how to shave I was initially worried that he'd cut off an important face part. "Has anybody seen my left dimple? It was here a minute ago."

This was an area I'd been an expert in for decades. By my midteen years I had grown whiskers on my cheeks, and the no-man's-land under my nose perpetually appeared to be dirty. Throw in my bushy blond sideburns, and I looked like a backup singer for ABBA.

"Jim, show him how to shave," my mother instructed my father at least three dozen times before he summoned me to the bathroom. My dad set a can of Barbasol on the sink, turned the water up hot, loaded a palm full of foam, and slathered it on his face. Finally he picked up his razor, the kind they simply don't make anymore—it weighed half a pound, and twisting the handle opened the top like a drawbridge. That was how you'd install a standard double-sided razor blade, the same killer my mother always warned us our neighbors would hide in candied apples on Halloween, which would rip our guts apart and cause a slow painful death unless our parents first inspected our treats.

"I like to start up here," my father said, pulling at his right sideburn, then cutting the first swath of stubble.

Back then my father was a bit of a fashion plate, with rakish sideburns that went with his groovy seventies hairdo. I thought they were Engelbert Humperdinckish, but not long ago my children saw a photo from that era and observed, "Check out Grandpa's muttonchops!"

I memorized the scraping sequence because I would be next. While I'd seen him do it hundreds of times, now I noticed how far he bent his nose over to the left so that he could get really close to the right of the nose, how he pulled the loose skin adjacent to his Adam's apple from one side to the other. Less than ninety seconds after he started he had whacked off everything that once grew on his face. At that moment I watched him rinse off the foam to reveal that he was bleeding from half a dozen new gouges. It was less personal hygiene and more a blood donation.

"Hand me that toilet paper, Stephen."

I can honestly say I don't remember ever seeing my dad leave the bathroom without at least one bit of dangling tissue paper used to clot and stop the blood, only to be yanked off later, which would start the bleeding all over again.

"Okay, Stephen, you're up."

The water was scalding, the mirror foggy. I pushed the button on the shaving cream, not realizing that more stuff comes out than you could possibly ever use. I applied a clownishly thick layer of shaving cream, and I thought to myself this was what Santa would look like if instead of whiskers, his beard was Cool Whip.

"Be careful, it's sharp," my dad said, handing me his shaver. I felt like such a man following exactly his sequence of strokes. I went from under my right ear down to my jaw and along the way lopped off the head of a zit, which announced its location with a scary stream of O-negative.

"Welcome to the club," the elder bleeder said to his son. I smiled a big grin that showed my teeth were positively yellow compared with the ultrabright white foam on my face. By the end of my virgin shave, I had a random series of scrapes and future scars. Detainees leave Gitmo with fewer contusions.

"Here, slap on a little of this" was the last thing I heard before my two palms damp with Mennen aftershave sent electric jolts of sheer pain into the subsurface of my face. I looked into the mirror expecting to see the hairdo of a Lhasa apso that had electrodes placed on its private regions, but from the outside you could not see my pain.

"That wasn't so bad, was it?" my dad asked as he opened the medicine chest to replace his razor, which was clearly on loan from the bloodmobile. I was officially a shaver; the torch had been passed. Okay, it was a bloody, scary torch, but nonetheless a milestone in my life. I sat down on the edge of the bathtub to relish my achievement, which was helpful because I was also a little light-headed from the massive loss of blood.

My father told my mom to buy me my own razor, either because he didn't want to share or was afraid he'd catch a crazy dose of hep C from my time hanging around down on the docks. Try as she might, she could not locate the same kind of razor my father had, probably because it was banned under the Geneva Conventions.

Instead, she picked up something that was new to the market, the disposable plastic razor. One difference between the little blue Bic razors and my father's hand-held Cuisinart was that the Bics never cut my face. Not the first time, nor the second, not on the third or ninth. That's when I deduced that perhaps my father's daily shrapnel wounds were from a world-class rusty blade. To this day I cannot remember him ever changing the blades in his razor, not once, which could explain why he always emerged from the bathroom looking like an extra from a Quentin Tarantino film.

Given my personal history, when it was time to teach my son how to shave, I bought him an electric shaver. I'd never had one of them, but I always liked the Norelco Christmas commercials and the way that jolly old elf shaved the snowy hills around the North Pole. Besides, after what had happened to me as a child, I didn't want a single divot on that adorable face of my stubbly boy. I had been worried about him using electricity so close to the sink, but as it turned out it was completely battery operated and with an adjustable pivoting head for a close and comfortable shave at an amazing 13,000 rpm. He could shave for three weeks and still have plenty of battery power to give Sasquatch a "Yul Brynner" with the pop-up trimmer.

Even though I had never used an electric, I had plenty of advice, because a lack of knowledge has never stopped a father from lecturing.

"Rub it all over your face wherever there's a whisker." To this day he has never emerged from the shavatorium looking like his grandfather, with an incurable case of toilet-paper pox.

This is what we do as fathers. We teach not only with our words, but also by our example. I have great personal satisfaction knowing that the things that I've passed along to my son are helpful and safe. Actually, the only way he could possibly get hurt would be if he dropped his electric shaver into the giraffe toilet while standing over it, but I don't see that happening, since we sold the giraffe at a garage sale in 1996.

12

My Father

Jim Dandy

Most kids are, at some point in their childhood, embarrassed by their parents. My father was not an astronaut, the president of a bank, or an automobile dealer with his name memorialized in cursive chrome on the rear ends of legions of Buicks, and I felt that revealing that he was a traveling salesman would be too ordinary for my bloodline, so I invented a far better biography.

"What's your dad do, Steve?"

"We don't like to spread it around," I'd whisper, before divulging a well-kept family secret: "but my dad is the guy who invented the artificial heart, which is also dishwasher safe."

"Cool," they'd respond, not asking the follow-up question: "Then why's he drive a Ford pickup with a feed-company name on it?"

Later I realized that such an outrageous exaggeration was problematic when I admitted to a really cute college girl from Florida, "My father invented Teflon."

"Your dad is Dr. Roy Plunkett?" The chemistry major who'd just studied Teflon in class seemed positively giddy that she was in the presence of chemistry royalty.

"Did I say Teflon? I meant the Chia Pet," I backtracked, because to the best of my knowledge nobody had taken credit for that.

In reality, I should have just told them the truth about my dad because it was a much better story. There was perhaps a reason why Jim Doocy would become the funniest guy I've ever known: he was born on April Fools' Day 1933, smack-dab on his mother's kitchen table—what some people would do to avoid a copay. But on the kitchen table? Imagine that dinner conversation. "Mama, would you move your leg a little to the left, I can't get the peas and carrots."

The second of seven children, my father was raised in north central Iowa at the end of the Great Depression, which meant that when I was growing up he'd roam room to room flipping off the light switches, reminding no one in particular, "Do you know how much that's costing me?" We did not, nor did we care. We were kids. My father's dad was 100 percent Irish, a large and bald dirt farmer who taught his farmhand children how everything worked, starting with how to correctly milk a cow.

"Hey, Phil, where'd you get that horn hole in your forehead?"

"Milked the bull . . . briefly."

Grandpa Doocy started his family late in life when he married at fifty. He was nearing retirement age when my father was growing up, so my dad's mother was left to get things done. I remember Sundays after church when I was a little boy. She'd say, "Stephen, come help me with dinner," and we'd walk around to the backyard, where she'd sneak up behind one of the two dozen penned-up chickens, grab one by the leg, and haul it clucking and flailing over to a weathered stump, where she'd nonchalantly pick up a little hatchet, and in a single movement that required precision every time, she'd whack the head off the chicken.

My eyes were always clamped closed at the moment, but as soon as I'd hear the thump on the stump I'd open them up because for the next ten to fifteen seconds the headless chicken body would run around the backyard willy-nilly.

"They're so dumb, they don't know they're dead yet," she'd say as I'd watch until the chicken would run out of gas, keel over, and become an entrée.

"Stephen, grab me another," she'd call out.

Come on, Grandma. The entire flock just watched their cousin go to that big KFC in the sky. If I got too close they'd give me the Tippi

Hedren treatment. But because it was an order not a request, I'd walk up to within a yard of the hens, never closer, and announce in a loud voice, "Here, chicken . . . chick . . . chick . . .," a pathetic attempt. I never closed the deal. Grandma'd always bring home the bacon, doing the Marie Antoinette number, and after another headless crazy chicken dance our Sunday dinner preparation was complete.

"Stephen, put the heads in the trash can" is something you don't hear much these days. I prayed back then that a neighborhood dog or a wandering band of hoboes would beat me to that chore.

My dad grew up a good student, a hard worker, and a terrific baseball player. He had a part-time job after school at the local pool hall, where he famously taught the nuns from his high school how to play pool. The other noteworthy thing he did before age twenty, he died.

His mother thought he'd come down with the flu, so he stayed home and they nursed him, not knowing that his appendix had burst and poison that would kill him was spreading through his body. When he was at death's door they took him to the hospital. "He won't make it through the night," his parents were told, so a priest was called to give last rites to my unconscious father. Shortly after the last rites, he woke up, and then over a few days he completely recovered. Was it a miracle or just good timing? I believe in my heart it was a little of both—he wasn't supposed to make it through the night. Maybe the priest arrived at just the divine moment he rounded a corner, making an amazing coincidence. My own parish priest tells me that a coincidence is God's way of working anonymously.

He had to get better or I never would have been born, because twenty miles south of my father's hometown of Bancroft, Iowa, is Algona, where my mother, a pretty woman named JoAnne Sharp, lived in a tiny house on a huge lot that smelled of rhubarb and lilacs in the summer. Her mother, Lilly, a second-generation Swede, raised her and her sister, Linda, on a tiny income as a short-order cook at a highway greasy spoon called Frank and Em's. I honestly don't know what her father did; for most of my life, he lived a solitary life in an Airstream trailer parked in Wickenburg, Arizona, because the weather was better. Their family name was Sharp, and I'm hoping that one day soon a lawyer with a Halliburton aluminum attaché case filled with unmarked bills will knock on my door to inform me that my little-known grandfather founded Sharp electronics, and I'm the sole heir. This theory is, however, highly unlikely, because I remember him asking me when I was five, "Do you know to change the channels?" as he sat in his easy chair and drank room-temperature Grain Belt beer he kept under the stove.

When my father's older brother Phil came back from serving in the marines in Korea, he was introduced to his future wife, Jane, by a pretty blonde who worked with her at the water department. That woman just happened to be her next-door neighbor and best friend, my mother. Something mysterious clicked on my parents' first date, because after a few short months my mother and father were engaged, and they married the next June. Less than a year after they got hitched my father was drafted into the United States Army and shipped out for basic training; when he left, he didn't know that his new wife was pregnant.

One generation later, when I was of age, I registered for military service but was told that because I had a heart murmur, I was disqualified. Wanting to continue the family tradition of service to our nation, I convinced the recruiter to classify me 7-F, which meant that in the event of conflict, I was to be immediately taken as a human shield.

My father had never traveled far from home, so the army was his chance to see the world. First stop Fort Carson, Colorado, then to White Sands Testing Grounds, and later a troop train transported him to Brooklyn, where he was placed on a troop transport, the SS *Geiger*, for a very rough passage across the North Atlantic, so while my mother was morning sick, my father was seasick. He volunteered to work in the mess hall, where he learned from a PFC named George that the fastest way to peel potatoes was to bake them, cut them, then put them on the floor and stomp on them with his combat boots to make the skins come off. George was eventually dismissed from the kitchen, and my father stopped eating anything prepared by a man in camouflage.

Deployed to the Black Forest of Germany, Dad wound up working as a supply guy, making sure the men of the Twenty-third Anti-aircraft Artillery Battalion had plenty of sleeping bags, lanterns, and gas masks. He was not in charge of weapons, which was fine by him because nobody ever accidentally killed himself when he dropped a gas mask.

At that same time my mother was stateside and worked as an executive secretary at Snap On Tools, which sounds like a marital aid business but was in fact a tool company that sold tools that snapped on.

For his service, once a month Dad would get a twenty-eight-dollar check from the United States Treasury, and another was sent to my mom for about a hundred bucks. It was during his overseas duty that I was born, and my father remembers his commanding officer's exact words when the CO called him to the base headquarters: "Private Doocy, you're a father. Congratulations." Being the family-friendly organization it was in the 1950s, the army promptly sent him home to see his wife and baby, eighteen months later.

"Look what I've missed!" he said when he first laid eyes on me. "Is he shaving yet?" The humor was probably lost on my mother, who'd spent a year and a half waiting for her husband to come home to kill a very large bug in the bathroom.

After his service, my mom and dad and I retired to our family compound, a thousand-square-foot shotgun house at the end of Wooster Street, in Algona. The good news was it was not on the wrong side of the tracks; the bad news was it was literally on the side of the tracks. Barely a hundred feet from my bedroom window, the vibration from the Soo Line freight trains woke me up in the middle of the night and made my Lassie lamp shake like a hula dancer.

My mother retired from work and became a stay-at-home mom as my sisters, Cathy and Lisa, were born. My dad started a string of jobs. The first was chicken doctor. Sent to Iowa State University to learn how to diagnose chicken ailments for a huge poultry hatchery. Whenever a local farmer had a sick bird, he'd call my dad to make sure it wasn't something really bad. Luckily, my father never took his mother to work with him. "This one has a sore throat," he'd say, milliseconds before Grandma'd get out her hatchet and chop the head off of one of her son's clients. *Case closed. Let's eat.*

Aside from the train tracks at the end of the street, it was not a normal neighborhood. One woman down the block had a Technicolor-tinted hairdo that seemed a hundred watts brighter than Lucille Ball's. One night when my mom was busy, the redhead invited my father and me over for dinner. I remember my father saying on the way there, "Don't talk, just listen."

"Hello, Jim, Stevie, come on in," she said as she escorted us into the dining room, where a huge banquet was being served. Ten place settings were already piled high with dinner. Our hostess sat at one end of the table, talking to guests on her left and right, encouraging them to eat more. The perfect hostess. But there was one problem— besides my father, me, and the redhead, the room was empty. Plates stayed filled with untouched food as the chatty woman spoke directly at empty chairs. I wanted to whisper to my dad for an explanation but radio silence had been imposed.

"Marvin, how's Thelma?" she asked, and then stared at her imaginary friend Marvin, nodding along to whatever the nonexistent diner was saying. It was my first experience with an obviously crazy person, but it prepared me for a career in talk television.

Around my fifth birthday, I drove with my mother, and heard a radio news story about how a couple of killers went into a Kansas farmhouse and murdered an entire family. Truman Capote wound up doing a book on it called *In Cold Blood.* As my mother listened to the stories about the killing on the radio, I remember her saying, "Strange things happen out there. I wouldn't move to Kansas for a million dollars."

Within a week my father came home with exciting news: "We're moving to Kansas!"

My mom did not get a million reasons to move, just one: a friend of my father's had offered him a job in ad sales where the entire state would be his territory, and it seemed like a great career move. But to me it seemed like a gamble to trade our little house on the tracks for a little house on the prairie. Once in our new house I had trouble adjusting, probably because every time the doorbell rang after dark, I thought it was Dick and Perry there to string us up in the basement, demanding to know the whereabouts of our priceless antiquities.

With my dad covering eighty thousand square miles of sales territory, he was gone a lot, but he always found time to get home, as evidenced by the fact that it was during this time that my sisters Ann and Jennifer were born. On weekends he tried to make up for his absence by taking us on little trips. I remember walking the streets of an authentic frontier street called Old Abilene Town, with my cap gun drawn in case a bank robber or horse thief needed to get pumped full of lead, and my dad pointed to the stenciled name along the top of the stagecoach: BUTTERFIELD OVERLAND STAGE COMPANY.

"Kids, that's our family . . . I think."

That sent shock waves through our family—we'd never known we might be related to anything close to a transit system. We listened as he explained that a family named Butterfield adopted his mother, the chicken whisperer. They were childless until the orphan train came to town. From the Civil War through the early twentieth century, a number of Eastern big-city orphanages organized and transported entire trains full of kids into the Midwest. The trains would pull up to a town and people would gather around to see if they had a child on board who would fit into their family tree.

"Do you have anything in a redhead with green eyes?"

If they did, papers were signed and the kid made that town his or her home. Frank Butterfield and his wife, Ida Blood Butterfield, picked my grandma off the train, which was like a Polar Express with people.

Ida was a full-blooded Cherokee Indian, and it never occurred to me until just now typing this out that I have spent my life incorrectly checking the box that identifies me as White/Caucasian, when in fact I could almost truthfully check the Sort of Native American box.

There was a big problem for a family man with a job as a traveling salesman. He was gone a lot. He missed a lot of school events, birthdays, and my entire American Legion baseball career. My mom hated it, and apparently so did he, because one day he announced that he'd had enough, and quit to do something he'd always wanted, carpentry work, which he taught himself thanks to some books at the public library. We were happy to have Dad at home, but also terrified that we would wind up in the poorhouse, as wards of the state, or shipped off on an orphan train for children of the unemployed. But he assured us we'd be fine.

We ate a lot of ten-for-a-dollar pot pies, and my mother learned how to stretch a budget because by the end of the week all that would be left in the fridge would be a loaf of bread and a pound of hamburger. She'd toast the bread, fry the meat, and make a surprisingly tasty gravy for what my dad said they called SOS in the army. Once midmeal I made the mistake of asking what SOS stood for, and much to my horror, he told me. The "on a shingle" part didn't faze me; it was the first *S* that scared me into eating just the toast and gravy, until my mother renamed it "chipped beef on toast."

We did struggle when I was growing up. We never had a new car or a big house. But as kids we didn't know we were missing them, because everybody we knew was in the same boat. Looking back now I know that we were actually a poorer version of *Angela's Ashes*. Compared with us, Frank McCourt lived like Steve Forbes.

When I was in college I made up stories about what my dad did. I guess I was embarrassed by what other people would think. Now that I'm older I feel bad about that and know how unfair it is that some people look at a person's job as a yardstick of success. A doctor gets an automatic ten-yard advantage on the field of life over an auto mechanic regardless of the lives they've led. My dad has had a bunch of jobs over his life, never big jobs, to anybody but us. He never made a million dollars or did anything that would have had his face plastered in *BusinessWeek* or on *Entertainment Tonight*. The closest thing to momentary fame happened when he visited me at Fox News.

I'd left him in the greenroom during our three-hour program, and he entertained the upcoming guests with stories about me that only a proud parent could get away with. During a commercial I walked by and saw he was regaling the actress Donna Mills with an apparently hilarious story. She was standing ever so close, and my father had a mischievous grin as the cute woman from *Knots Landing* hung on his every word.

I couldn't stop to talk; I was heading outside for an interview with football legend Joe Namath. The New York Jets' only Super Bowl–winning quarterback was mythical in Manhattan. During the interview passersby stopped until they were ten deep to watch Broadway Joe. Suddenly we were creating a security problem. The crowd was huge, and people were getting pushed into rush-hour traffic. Midway through our televised chat, a guy unexpectedly walked up and stood about six inches from Joe Namath's left arm. Normally our security detail would have stopped the man from getting on camera, but on that day they made an exception because the interloper was my father.

"Joe, that's my dad, Jim," I broadcast as the camera panned over to see my old man with a big goofy grin on his face, practically standing on Joe's foot.

"Jim," Namath started, "you must be proud of this boy of yours."

"Why has your father hijacked the program?" the producer screamed in my earpiece.

"Dad," I interrupted their chitchat, "is there *a reason* you stopped by?"

Two authentic NFL footballs were pulled out of a plastic shopping bag along with a Sharpie. "Joe, would you mind signing a ball for a church auction and another for my grandson?"

My father, the most honest guy I know, wanted them signed on television to authenticate to the bidders at St. Andrew's Catholic

Church that the ball was really signed by Mr. Namath, who was the perfect gentleman and scrawled his name and jersey number on it. Later the producer said the segment was hilarious. "Could your dad come back and do that again tomorrow?"

After the show I walked into the greenroom, and there were my dad and Namath laughing up a storm like a couple of frat brothers. It made me feel good that I could give my dad a chance to chew the fat with a bona fide football hero, who, I might add, seemed genuinely happy to share the couch with my father. One of our college-aged interns looking in would probably just see a couple of old guys sharing a laugh, but I saw two legends.

One guy made millions throwing a ball; the other guy never got that big break, didn't get to go to college, and worked hard and long until his back gave out. But his spirit never did.

I have had the pleasure of meeting and working with some giants of modern American history, but for heroism nobody ever got close to Jim Doocy, my biological father, a gentleman who once carried an autographed football on his lap across the country so he could present it to his grandson, who had no idea what a Joe Namath was.

13

Humor

The Joker Gene

The five-hundred-mile drive to Grandma's house in northern Iowa was mind-numbingly dull. My mother invented a time killer called "What am I thinking about," which usually lasted ten minutes before my younger sisters lost interest because they didn't care what my mother was thinking about.

The halfway point was the Missouri River, which we'd cross on the triple-cantilevered Abraham Lincoln Bridge, as it is officially designated by the state of Nebraska. But we called it by the name of the town it sits next to, Blair, Nebraska.

"Fifty miles to the Blair Bridge," my dad would announce when he'd see a road sign for the state line. Just that announcement would start almost an hour of anxiety because for a family from the country's most landlocked state, a triple-span soaring bridge was scary.

"Twenty-seven miles to the Blair."

The closer we got to the bridge, the more the tone of Dad's announcements changed. First they were simply informational; then as we got closer things would get more foreboding. There was one more petrifying component to my dad's little soap opera; the bridge deck was made of a metal mesh that made an ominous sound as you crossed.

Mummummummmum.

The faster Dad drove, the higher the pitch, and the louder and scarier the sound the bridge sang to us.

AAAAAMMMMMMMMM.

"Three minutes," he announced. "Hang on!" He started sounding like the NASA guy whose job it was to count backward: "T-minus one minute and counting . . ."

"Jim, stop it," my mother said. He never did.

As the car angled up the long steep approach, my sisters and I would crouch down in the back so we didn't have to watch, and to this day I can remember closing my eyes and praying that it would be fast. Keep in mind, this was about the time the movie *The Poseidon Adventure* was in theaters, and our car flying into the river seemed as plausible as Shelley Winters hanging by a chandelier upside down in a ballroom as Maureen McGovern sang, "There's got to be a morning after . . ."

AAMMMAAAAHHHHHHHHHEEEEERRR.

The sound and the height combined to quicken our little hearts, but that was never enough for our dad; always midspan, at the height of our personal peril, he would swerve a little. On some trips he'd throw his hands up in the air like people on roller coasters do, steering with his knees. Of course we'd never see that, because our eyes would have to be pried open first.

"Kids, we made it!" he would announce with the same satisfied voice Chuck Yeager would use after a successful test flight of some eminently dangerous flying contraption.

In reality all that we'd done was cross a bridge that was probably thirty feet above the Missouri, which at that location was probably as deep as Paris Hilton.

The reason my dad did that every time we'd cross it was he thought it was comical, yet to this day his joke haunts us all. Today my sisters and I all get sweaty palms at the thought of crossing a bridge. Unfortunately for me, a really big one stands between me and a paycheck, the George Washington Bridge, one of the country's longest, highest, and ultimately scariest bridges. A bridge-fear expert once suggested I drive across it wearing a puffy orange Coast Guard-approved life jacket, which I did as a joke until the Port Authority police stopped me because they thought I was wearing a belt bomb.

Not long ago I asked my father if he realized that he'd permanently freaked out his entire family, and he played the humor card. "I was just trying to be funny."

I said nothing, letting him twist a little.

"Listen, if I wanted to scare you, I would have worn shorts to the pool."

My father was simply keeping up the time-honored tradition of the dad as tickler of the family funny bone. He has since passed down his big clown shoes to me.

After taking my kids to see the movie *Toy Story*, where Mr. Potato Head and Barbie come alive, that evening while tucking my four-year-old-daughter Mary into her bed I said, "Don't forget, toys really do get sad when you don't play with them." And then I pointed around the room at the legions of mute toys waiting to play. A kiss good night, I turned off her light, and instantly forgot about my little joke.

Nine years later, over dinner, Mary blurted out that when I told her toys got lonely unless she played with them, she started spending ten, fifteen, sometimes twenty minutes a night kissing each one. If she heard somebody in the hall she'd jump into bed, and when it was time to resume the kissing she'd forgotten her place and would have to start over.

"I was joking" was my only defense, but that did little to remedy my attempt at humor, which tortured her for years. She's now in college, and I believe she's over it, but if she needs to speak to anybody professionally, I'll get her some therapy as soon as Dr. Joyce Brothers opens an office at the Garden State Plaza next to the Sprint kiosk.

I would officially like a do-over on the *Toy Story* kissing incident.

Despite the fact that my own father's sense of humor tinged me, *for three decades,* he still makes us all laugh. My sister and her brand-new husband of five minutes were posing at the altar for their final wedding photographs when somebody noticed that my daughter

Sally the flower girl was making a strange sound. It wasn't exactly a hack, but more of a cough, short and wheezy. Initially it didn't register as anything other than a little bark until her eyes got glassy and we realized she wasn't breathing.

"Did she eat the flower bouquet?" No.

"Is she too young for the Heimlich?" Probably.

Somebody suggested we give her a drink, which seemed like a bad idea to me, and it was about that time that Sally started crying. She couldn't breathe, but she could cry, and she was simultaneously turning blue. For someone choking to death she was remarkably calm. As we stood there playing Twenty Questions, she started a series of gut-wrenching dry coughs until, just like a cat belting out a fur ball, she sent a projectile flying two feet straight out of her mouth. It wasn't a flower or a piece of candy. It was a quarter.

"Thank God she's all right!" the bride exclaimed, and this was followed by a round of "Amens."

Crisis averted, my sister Ann the caterer asked, "Who wants cake?" and we adjourned to the parish hall. We were not inclined to blame whoever had left the quarter on the floor of Our Lady of the Immaculate Kitchen.

The next day Sally climbed up on my dad's lap. She seemed a little lower key because she'd learned a lesson: "Don't eat da money." She repeated her new mantra to her grandfather. "Don't eat da money."

"That's right, don't eat the money." Then my father, Mr. Catskills, went back to work. "Sally, do me a favor. How about coughing up another quarter? Grandpa needs a newspaper."

14

Independence

Driving Miss Doocy

"See, it's like a triple-legged *H*." My father pointed to the top of the gearshift during my first driving lesson. The family car was a 1963 Plymouth Belvedere that my father had bought from a friend who had used it as a stock car. Most people get their first taste of the road in a vehicle that's "street legal"; I, on the other hand, learned how to drive in a car that had, next to the license plate, a parachute.

"It's a little souped-up, so let's take it easy," my dad said after a thorough thirty-second orientation. When I turned over the ignition I immediately heard the deep throaty *lub-dub-dub-dub* of a 427-horsepower gas-guzzler modified to feature "double carbs," which had nothing to do with the Atkins diet.

My father taught me the basic tenets of driving over half a dozen afternoons on little-used dirt roads where the land was flat and the cops were few and far between. In Kansas, if you were involved in some branch of agriculture, you could obtain a "farm duty" driver's license at age thirteen and a half, which was my age at that moment, so I applied for and got one. Being honest, to justify the license my parents made me find an actual farm job, which wasn't hard, because farmers were always searching for young men to work on impossibly hot days, slowly squeezing the life out of them.

One phone call and I had a two-dollar-an-hour job. But it did not require a license. I stood on a slow-moving hay wagon, grabbing hay bales as they shot out of a baling machine. Halfway through the first day I pulled out a fresh bale of alfalfa that seemed *noisy* for hay. I thought the buzzing was the sound of a bee until I saw the tail of a rattlesnake. If the hay-bale hurl had been an Olympic competition that year, I would have advanced immediately to the semifinals. And folks wonder why kids leave the family farm for the bright lights of Omaha.

Seeing that I was freaked out, the farmer asked me if I'd like to change places with him and drive the tractor. My back was broken and I was thoroughly exhausted; when he offered to switch jobs I had the same sense of liberation that Jessica Lynch probably felt when those marines showed up and rescued her from that hospital.

"Do you know how to drive a hand clutch?" he asked.

"Sure do," I said, having no idea what he was talking about, but how hard could it be? He could do it, and he clearly wasn't the sharpest tool in the barn. *(FYI: sharpest tool in the barn, the pitchfork.)*

I climbed into the driver's seat and was suddenly presiding over the tractor, which was towing a baler and a hay wagon; I was the conductor of my first three-vehicle parade. The hand clutch did the same thing as a foot-pedal clutch, but they'd installed it up by the steering wheel, apparently just to make it more precarious.

"Just let the clutch out slowly," the farmer told me as I maneuvered a hand throttle with my right hand, speeding up the tempo of the tractor, while slowly releasing the hand clutch in my left hand. With both hands busy, I theorized that drivers had to steer with their pelvis, the only available body part approximate to the wheel. The space shuttle had simpler controls than this contraption, which really was a slow-moving lawsuit: fifty linear feet of gas-powered mechanized hardware, dangerous and lethal, with whirling sharp parts and random yellow warning stickers—"To Lose Finger Touch Here." Perhaps the danger level was why they had resorted to "hand clutches," because after a few harvest seasons farmers had already lopped off their feet and legs, and hand clutches allowed them to continue to harvest crops while missing a limb or two.

"You can speed up a little," the farmer yelled.

Immediately I followed my captain's order and throttled up to four miles an hour. As I made a three-quarter turn the farmer pointed to the starboard side in the direction of a twenty-foot-wide swath of grass that I'd simply missed.

"Back up!" he yelled. I immediately throttled down the gas, pushed in the brake and the clutch, and finally disengaged the power takeoff to the baler. The whole shebang stopped. "Can you back up?"

"Sure," I lied.

Backing a tractor is one thing, but a tractor with two other things hitched behind it is something that causes professional drivers with twenty years of experience to lie on the floor in the fetal position screaming, "Don't make me, don't make me!"

If I told him I couldn't do it, I would relinquish my seat on the tractor and have to lift another ton of hay bales, so using the wisdom of a thirteen-year-old, I thought, How hard can it be? I shifted into reverse gear, gave it some gas with one hand, and then slowly released the hand clutch with the other, but because I was looking backward, I got mixed up. Within seconds the tractor jackknifed over the baler and I heard the nauseating sound of sheet metal ripping and factory installed rivets popping. The trailer hitch was pretzelized, and the power takeoff had flown off and hurled in the direction of the rattlesnake hay bale. It was like a Lee Marvin film, although if it had been a movie, the thing would have killed the snake family, but during the editing stage PETA would have petitioned to have the producers take out the pain and suffering of the rattlesnake and replace it with something made of tofu.

His agriculture armada destroyed, the farmer issued a brief statement. "I think we're done for today."

I never told my children about that John Deere disaster. However, long before the kids were ready to drive I taught them all an important lesson regarding handicapped parking spaces.

After one of my wife's knee surgeries she got a temporary handicapped hangtag courtesy of those bighearted bureaucrats at the Division of Motor Vehicles. Three years earlier our golden retriever, Charlie, had shot out of the house like a blond bullet and jumped up at my wife, spinning her around with such force that the torque of the abrupt turn shattered her kneecap. Never once a complainer and certainly not one to get rid of the dog, over time she'd have five surgeries and then a total knee replacement. It was awful. On the bright side, with her temporary handicapped pass, she could park closer to the mall door than any of her friends, because she'd spent more time on crutches than Evel Knievel.

Heading to Christmas-shop at Target, where we would purchase large quantities of quality American products at reasonable prices, she asked me to park in a handicapped spot, but they were all taken, so I headed toward the door where I would drop off her and the kids. Then I spotted a shopper with absolutely no visible physical problem practically skipping back to his car in the handicapped section. Clearly he was physically perfectly fine, and really should have been ashamed that he was using sick Aunt Thelma's parking tag. Just as he pulled out of his spot, as I inched toward the opening, the same kind of van as in the Cheech and Chong movies careened around the corner and lunged to a stop in the spot.

"*Hey!* That space belongs to me!" I barked, and then backpedaled. "I mean, that's your mother's space." Nothing agitates a mall crawler more than having a good spot snatched away. Then I made a snap decision; I parked the car right there in traffic and bolted out the door to give the handicapped-parking thief a lecture.

"What are you doing, Dad?" the kids asked, but I was single-minded as I walked toward the van, which had no handicapped plate, no official state hangtag, no permit, just a bumper sticker that read "I'm Not Gaining Weight, I'm Retaining Food."

This should be good, I thought. My kids will see me sticking up for their mother. With the bass line of a Marilyn Manson song thumping from the van, when the driver saw me in his rearview, he lowered the volume and his window, and I was face-to-face with a midforties guy as something that smelled like incense rolled out. "Hey, buddy, these spots are here for people like my wife." I pointed toward my bride, who gave a little nod, and suddenly I was Lancelot, defending the honor of my Guinevere.

"Your *wife* needs it?"

"She does, and she's got the parking hangtag," I said, pointing to the red-and-white placard bearing the international symbol for "Park Close to the Store."

"Too freaking bad!" he blared, his surly demeanor having instantly metastasized into naked anger. He then pivoted in his seat commando style and reached down to grab what the sinking feeling in my gut knew was either a sawed-off shotgun or an RPG launcher.

"Your wife needs it? Well have her talk to my little friend!" he spat in my direction.

He was aiming it squarely at my chest. Please tell me I'm dreaming, I prayed as I stared down the barrel of a prosthetic leg.

"Tell your wife I got here first, and possession is nine-tenths of the law!"

Horrified, speechless, and suddenly humiliated, I wondered, Where is his handicapped tag or permit? "I am sorry, sir, please accept my apologies."

"It's people like you," he shrieked, but I'd stopped listening to the words and it came out just blah, blah, blah. It was a cockamamie idea to approach him in the first place, so I stood there and took my medicine like a man. Eventually he ran out of steam and I returned to our car. From watching their official male role model get chewed out by a guy with high blood pressure and a factory-built limb, my observant heirs learned that day that only a nincompoop approaches a total stranger in New York State and asks him to relinquish a primo parking spot.

My son, Peter, was an eyewitness to that event, and I knew he would not repeat the mistakes of his father, who was in charge of the family motor pool and driving lessons. A veteran of stock cars and farm implements, I wanted to instruct him just as my father had done for me; however, state law said that every student driver had to spend six hours scaring the daylights out of somebody from a professional drivers school, not a blood relative, so my wife enrolled him for the mandatory three sessions. Upon successful completion of the class, Peter received a nonbinding, nonlegal, nondriver's certificate that was also good for 10 percent off at Jiffy Lube.

Assured that he was fully prepared for his upcoming DMV road test, I discovered during a practice joyride that despite the certificate and the three-hundred-dollar price tag, little attention had been paid to things like those red octagonal signs, one of which my son drove past at twenty-five miles an hour.

"Stop sign!" I yelled in a scary loud voice that I'd promised I'd never use, but did because I thought we were going to die.

The driving school had been a motorized babysitter at fifty dollars and fifty miles an hour. Since it had not worked, I happily resumed the role of family motor pool instructor. Following in my father's footsteps, I first quietly described where we would go and what maneuvers he'd work on (K-turn, parallel parking, merging). Once in motion, Peter almost instantly put us in peril, and again I was screaming like somebody who just discovered he'd consumed half of a dachshund smoothie.

After a month of neighborhood driving, he was ready for highway action. Near a mall I had him pull over and park at an IKEA store, where we celebrated surviving the drive with a fat-free yogurt. Ready to return home, we'd just exited the parking garage when he got a look of terror on his face—this would be his first time merging onto a very busy highway where cars were zipping by at sixty and better. Peter was edgy; I was positively damp. Waiting for ten, fifteen, thirty seconds for a clearing in the traffic that never came, he looked in his mirror and screamed.

"BUS!"

I turned and indeed a huge one was bearing down on us and in a split second would rear-end us into the highway traffic for instant and painless unscheduled deaths.

"Let's go," I firmly commanded. "Now, Peter!"

The blood had drained from his face just before we heard *the noise*. In the movies this is what Bruce Willis always hears just before his vehicle is totaled by an assassin/monster/asteroid. There are few things as terrifying before impact as the sound of an air horn.

HONNNNNNNNNNNNKKKKKccchhh!

We would soon be dead, and the papers the next day would let the world know that we had shopped at a cut-rate Swedish furniture store. Why couldn't it be outside of Saks Fifth Avenue?

SSSSSSQQQQUEEEKKKkkkk . . .

The air brakes, combined with some tread left on the bus tires, competently stopped the Metro vehicle a safe five centimeters from our rear bumper. Because I was in the backseat observing the driver, I turned around to give the uniformed state employee the stink eye. The New Jersey Transit driver in return glared back at me for having the audacity to stop between him and his union-mandated coffee break.

"PETER, LET'S GO!" You could hear the capitalization in my voice. "*NOW!*"

He nudged the gas and we lurched out into traffic, the bus passed us within ten seconds, and I spotted his number next to a "How's My Driving?" sign. I didn't call to complain, because in reality, I'd lost most of my voice and needed a lozenge.

Despite expensive driving-school lessons, a semester of high school classroom work, and my own personalized instruction, I sensed Peter's chances of passing the fast-approaching test were grim. He, however, was an optimist and had already made plans for his eighteenth birthday. First he'd ace his driver's test at the DMV, and then he'd drive directly to the one place he had apparently dreamed of driving up to, flaunting his newfound independence: Taco Bell.

"Gordita to go, my fine man!"

Finally, late in the afternoon, with his still-warm laminated license in his pocket, he was planning to drive a carful of friends to see the Dave Matthews Band in Camden, New Jersey, which for several years had the distinction of being the most dangerous city in America. That was his plan. That didn't happen. By a quarter after eleven on his eighteenth birthday, he'd already flunked his road test at the DMV, when he ran a stop sign and then exceeded the test track's posted speed limit, causing the examiner to mumble what sounded like a Hail Mary.

"This is not how it was supposed to work out!" he screamed as he slammed the door to his room. I was relieved. I didn't really want him driving seventy miles to a concert on his first day, and besides, what about the crime problem in Camden? How could I live with myself if my son accidentally ran over a carjacker?

After two more months of intensive screaming/instruction, I escorted my son to the Lodi, New Jersey, DMV, which was just a couple of curb cuts from Satin Dolls, which was used as the location for the Bada Bing strip joint in *The Sopranos*. But my son wasn't thinking lap dances, he was thinking lap belts. "Click it or ticket," the banner announced.

Peter's examiner was a very nice man who reviewed his previous exam and, being one last test away from quitting time, pointed into the middle distance and said, "Get me around that pole over there, and if you don't flip the car on the way back, you'll pass."

He passed, and we were understandably relieved, until our new car-insurance policy arrived and we discovered that the very large number near our name was not our zip code, but our new premium.

One of the things my father taught me I have passed on to my children. Whenever he'd brake too hard, he'd automatically stiff-arm his passenger back when seats were slippery and seat belts were still on the drawing board. Now when Peter drives and brakes too hard or too fast, he throws his arm to my chest to make sure I don't hit the dash. And once he knows I'm all right, he'll shove his hand into my wallet to get money for dinner and a show.

My daughter Mary was next, and a new drivers school was employed. A tall, patient man arrived one Tuesday afternoon for her first lesson. It was an out-of-body experience to see our little girl drive off into the sunset with a man in a dented Camry with STUDENT

DRIVER in humongous letters on the roof that could easily be viewed from Google Earth.

(Note to drivers schools: Maybe a dented car isn't the best advertising, unless your company slogan is "We haven't totaled one yet.")

Ninety minutes later, she returned with a breathless recapitulation of hair-raising stories of life on the road: initially terrified, she then found it exhilarating. Two more lessons and she graduated with honors and was presented with a certificate suitable for putting in a drawer and never looking at again.

Mary, Mary, was not contrary, but she was very conservative behind the wheel. She drove like a jumpy ninety-four-year-old woman who'd once forced a vanload of orphan cats and dogs off a mountain pass. Unlike her older sibling, she not only stopped at the red octagon sign but she spelled aloud "S-T-O-P," a trick her teacher taught her for timing an ample stop. Combine that drawn-out spelling with a bit of reluctance to mosey back into traffic, and in a New York minute the driver behind us laid on the horn because they didn't like waiting at a stop sign long enough to process a roll of film.

"Why is he honking?" She was frantically looking at the rearview.

"Because he's late for his anger-management class. Let's go."

On our last practice lap before her driving test, as we passed a stone church on a main drag in our town, a car zipped up behind and beeped its horn for us to speed up. Pulling down the passenger visor mirror, I observed that the tailgater had ratcheted up the pressure on my daughter and was now also flashing the high beams like the highway patrol. The horn honking, light flashing, and unsafe tailgating went on for five blocks, until we hit a red light, where the tailgater laid on the horn.

"Put it in park," I said, reflexively opening the door. "Don't move."

"Daddy, where are you going?"

Where was I going and what was I doing? Once I'd committed to jumping out like some hothead it occurred to me that the driver might have a perfectly good explanation for wanting us to hurry.

Maybe it was a volunteer firefighter heading to a fire, or it might be a longshoreman with a lead pipe.

Half expecting to see a member of an organized-crime family with a five o'clock shadow, I was surprised to see that all of this road rage was the work of a petite woman about thirty.

"Roll down the window," I mouthed, and pantomimed with a circular hand-cranking gesture to the figure behind the tinted glass. At first she pretended she didn't understand, so I repeated and waited.

"What's your hurry?" I asked in a painfully friendly way.

"I'm late. Your wife was going way too slow."

"First of all, that's my daughter, who is learning how to drive. If it were my wife she would have come back here by now and stuffed you like a manicotti."

She just sat their staring straight ahead waiting for the light to change. "Sorry, I was in a hurry."

"For . . ."

She paused.

"For . . . a Pilates class." Suddenly the ill-fitting Lycra getup made sense. My disgust duly registered, I gave her an eye roll and a full five-finger wave as I climbed back into my car. I wanted to say, "Forget Pilates, you need an abs class," but that would have been wrong. Funny, but just wrong.

Mary high-fived me, and I instructed her to drive exactly twenty miles an hour for the next half mile, slowing down to hit the next light so we'd roadblock the Lycra lady from making the class at the YMCA in time. We're good people, but there had to be a little payback.

Mary passed the test on her second try.

Reviewing my driver instructor record, I realize that I yelled too much with my son and was too laid back with my daughter; in other words I was first talk radio and then NPR without the tote bag.

I will not repeat those errors with my third and final child. On Sally's seventeenth birthday, when she is old enough to drive and every other kid in her class is at the DMV, I'm going to take her straight to the bank, where I shall withdraw one thousand dollars and press it squarely in her hand, and give her the best driving advice she'll ever need.

"When you have to go someplace, call a cab."

By then surely Bell Labs will have perfected an everyday jet belt and she won't have to worry about tailgaters, baling machines, or Pilates.

15

Sex

The Birds, the Bees, and the Rubber *What?*

After an exhausting day of dodging manatees in a friend's motorboat on the Intracoastal Waterway in Boca Raton, we returned to his house, where the children took turns washing off the salt water in an outdoor shower. My job in such a situation was to inventory my children's whereabouts, and I was doing just that when I realized two were missing. I opened a side door to the house, where I located Sally standing in the foyer staring up the stairs where her second-grade male classmate was prancing around twirling a large towel while completely naked.

Uh-oh.

I would describe what I was witnessing as a *shaky butt dance*. He was performing with wild abandon because he thought he had an audience of only one. Sally stood below cackling like someone who'd been trapped for a month in a nitrous oxide plant.

I understand the toddlers' urge to run around the house naked, but they were seven years old and way past that. An intervention was required as nature boy went nuts.

"Hi, guys, what's happening?" I announced from far stage left out of their sight.

"Oh, jeez!"

The pint-sized Chippendale stopped shaking his groove thing, grabbed his wet suit, and slammed a door behind him. That was eight years ago; today Sally does not think nudity is a laughing matter. Like a former chocoholic who has sworn off Godivas, she has morphed into our most modest of children, uncomfortably knocking at puberty's front door.

As a member of the varsity swim team, once out of the pool she instantly encases herself in an oversized towel so her Speedo boy teammates don't notice that she is a girl. Her clothes go over her swimsuit for the ride home as she soaks the seat. Dashing upstairs to the bathroom, where the curtains are drawn, the door is locked, and the lights are dimmed, she showers wearing her swimsuit. Once the stink of chlorine is gone, she adjourns to her bedroom wrapped in a terry-cloth burka. She shows as much skin as a Saudi Arabian Hooters.

This subject of children and sex is fraught with anxiety. Children want and need to know things just like their parents do, as long as they don't have to do the explaining. Two of Mary's high school classmates contracted meningitis, which sent us to the doctor for a prophylactic shot of vaccine. The kids were very sick, and Mary was as freaked out as I'd ever seen her. She was trembling in the examination room, with both arms around my neck. The doctor arrived and quizzed her on possible symptoms. She had none. I have been to the pediatrician with the kids a hundred times, but this was the first time I'd accompanied her as a high schooler. I immediately noticed a difference in the doctor's line of questioning from the days when she was still wearing Barney and Baby Bop underpants.

"Mary, is there any reason to believe you're pregnant?"

Modest and proper, she froze and said nothing. This was the first time the embarrassing topic of sex had been brought up in front of her father. I quickly turned translator: "She's not pregnant."

Not the sharpest scalpel in the shed, the doctor continued. "Dad, cover your ears. Mary, on a scale of one to ten, how sexually active are you?"

Mary was as embarrassed as I'd ever seen her. Meanwhile I wondered, On a scale of one to ten, how sexually active am I? A happily married father of three, was I a ten, or to approach the upper tier does one need to have a Mexican cartwheel on one's résumé? It seemed an inopportune time to ask the doctor a personal follow-up.

"Mary, you're fine, don't worry," the doctor said before he gave her the $175 shot, which was not covered by my company's health plan.

Back in the car, not a word was said about the distressing doctor talk. There were some things in life you simply don't joke about, like sex talk with children or how Mahmoud Ahmadinejad's open-collar look seemed to be based on Tom Cruise's in *Rain Man*.

Nobody in my family ever spilled the sex beans to me; I had to pick it up on the mean streets of Wakefield, Kansas, where due to a misunderstanding with my chemistry teacher I spent an hour reflecting on my chattiness at the conclusion of the school day. I had never been in detention before, and when selecting a seat to serve my sentence, I sat at a table near the far wall with two seniors.

One boy was dreamily recounting what sounded like a professional wrestling match the night before in the backseat of his Ford Maverick. I'd heard the name of the girl he was describing before, and I knew she was very popular with the upperclassmen, and as I listened, I learned why. As an eighth-grade boy, I had not yet been told by my father about the birds and the bees, and what I was learning in the library really had nothing to do with either birds or bees.

Until that moment I had no idea how sex worked, none whatsoever; the ever vigilant student, I barely batted an eyelash, drinking in every single disgusting detail, trying desperately to act nonchalant.

That is so gross, I kept thinking. No wonder he was in detention.

The clock hit five, we were released, and life as I knew it had changed in those sixty minutes. I'd gone into that study hall a carefree junior high school boy, and I walked out finally knowing what happened behind closed bedroom doors or on the hump in the back of a Detroit subcompact.

There was an unexpected chill in the air as I opened the school's front door. The sky didn't seem as bright, and I was no longer an innocent young man. My mom waited in the parking lot, and when I climbed in I could tell she was mad at me for the detention. Mad at me? After what I'd just learned I wanted to scream, "I know your secret! How could you?" The answer was obviously "easily" because I had four sisters.

The only detention I ever had in my life, and I think the Almighty sent me to that study hall that day so my father wouldn't have a nervous breakdown when he had to tell me about sex. Coincidence, as I've said, is God's way of working anonymously.

A dozen years later I was in the car with my parents and my fiancée, Kathy Gerrity, the day before our wedding. I had heard about sex, but I still had not gotten the Talk from my father, and the sex-talk hourglass was running out of sand.

"Dad, tomorrow's the honeymoon. Want to fill me in on anything?"

I watched the corners of his smile turn up into a mischievous smirk, but he chose to say nothing. However, the family's arbiter of good taste, my mom, was riding limo style and punctuated the momentary uneasiness with "Stephen, this is neither the time nor the place."

"It's now or never. . . ."

Irked, my mother knew she'd rue the day one of her children would ask about s-e-x, but she had an alibi. "Stephen, don't you remember we gave you that book that explained it all?"

What book? She kept an illustrated medical manual on a high shelf, and one time when I was sick at home I used it to look up strep throat, only to discover pictures of unknown body parts and an accompanying text written so drily that I returned to diseases of the throat. I stared blankly at my mom, who cut to the chase: "Remember, it had a rubber tree on the cover."

Rubber tree?

Then the long-term-memory floodgates opened. "You mean that book you gave me in fourth grade, from the Time-Life Collection?"

My mother nodded, knowing she'd fulfilled her parental duty by supplying me with a book with all the answers for all of my sex questions. The reason I didn't remember it at first was because it wasn't a sex book but one about plant reproduction. It had not an iota of actual carnal knowledge. The book she should have given me would have arrived in a brown paper wrapper and contained illustrations with humans, and had useful answers to foreplay questions like how much Brut can a man apply before a woman's eyes start to water like she was hit with tear gas?

My mother and father apparently felt they were off the hook and never mentioned the topic again. My fiancée was probably planning to bolt from the car at the next stoplight and run to the safety of a normal family, but sadly for the future bride, there were no stoplights in my town.

I made a mental pledge that day that if I was ever blessed with children, they would get the sex talk from their parents when it was time.

We did have children, and as soon as they were talking we wondered, How early should a responsible parent address sex? When my three-year-old son watched his naked sister squirm on the changing table, he found himself at eye level with a view of her bare bottom that he'd never noticed before. At that exact moment nature called and as she peed it ran down her bottom. *Eureka!* He realized for the first time that boys and girls have different plumbing.

"Mommy, where's her penis?"

Relying upon a parenting book that was clearly written by somebody who'd never had children, Kathy answered the question honestly and clinically. Pointing to the no-man's-land on the bottom of his sister, my wife gave him the lowdown.

"Peter, boys have penises and girls have vaginas."

His face screwed up a little as if she'd just described, strand by strand, the chemical makeup of DNA; it was clear all he'd heard was a new word that started with a *v*.

"Mom, I know we live in *Virginia*. Where's her penis?"

Virginia, vagina, let's call the whole thing off.

Kathy perfectly addressed the issue, answering his sex question honestly and directly. Within seconds it was in one ear and out the other as he moved on to worrying about a moth he spied outside the screen window that he was afraid would get into the house that night and eat his eyebrows.

The next day as my wife and children were in the checkout lane at Safeway, Peter watched Bob the checker ring up the groceries. Bob was having a nice conversation with my wife, who was carrying our new baby girl in a Snugli, and apparently Peter was feeling a little left out of the conversation, so he decided to join in.

"My sister has a penis in her butt."

Bob slowed down a moment to look directly at our eldest son. My wife said it got very warm in the store.

"Yesterday I saw a penis in her butt!"

Bob continued his stare of suspicion and probably pushed the secret button under the counter to alert child welfare authorities of a child predator in checkout line 3.

Bob was not a parent. He was a part-time produce guy who would have appreciated my mother's rubber-tree book. He didn't know that Peter had seen his sister peeing, with it running down her backside, or that Peter had been told that "boys have penises and girls have vaginas." Nor did he know that kids' brains work like martini shakers, adding up to the grocery store epiphany "My sister has a penis in her butt."

My wife could have explained what had happened, and Peter would surely have backed her up, but at that moment she didn't feel she owed it to the man who'd given her the identical stink eye when she inadvertently tried to cash an expired coupon for a dollar off Yoplait yogurt cups.

Peter's public comments and questions about sex lay dormant for seven years until the family was watching breakfast television during the impeachment testimony regarding Monica the "Clintern."

"What's oral sex?" Peter queried over Frosted Mini Wheats, repeating something he'd just heard the commentators mention.

The fastest-thinking spinmeister I've ever met, his mother an-

swered almost automatically. "Oral means talk," she said as he nodded. "So oral sex is when you *talk* about sex."

A fantastic and seemingly plausible answer, it shut him up until
later in the day when he probably told his classmates, "My poor parents, they don't know what oral sex is."

A funny thing happened on the way to the sex talk for my son. The
longer I waited to tell him, the harder and harder it got, until late
in his high school years I had the feeling that I would procrastinate
until I was face-to-face with my son in the coatroom at his wedding
reception, just before he got into the limo for his honeymoon in a
Poconos champagne-glass bathtub.

But then one day, it was time. Between my son's sophomore and
junior years in high school he and his cousin Dane would spend their
summer at Oxford, land of rampant beer drinking and girls with cute
Kate Winslet accents that boys dug. I had prepared in my head a
speech that stressed abstinence, and would ask him, if he ever met
a girl and fell in love with her and then engaged in the "whole nine
yards," what would be left for the next date, a kidney transplant?

For this superdelicate, once-in-a-lifetime father-son talk, I chose
the intimate and confidential location of Yankee Stadium. Sometime
around the seventh-inning stretch, I decided it was time as we sat
there in a cone of silence, surrounded by forty-eight thousand drunk
guys.

"Listen, Peter, while you're away you may find yourself . . ." That
was as far as I got.

"Dad, don't."

"Things may happen—"

"We don't have to talk about this now." He squirmed.

"There are things you haven't seen on cable—"

"Please, Dad, stop it!"

"Why?"

"They explained it all in health class, okay?"

The sweaty palms, the seventeen-year fear that he'd hear what
it was all about and the sky would darken as had happened to me,

all that for naught? It was true, thanks to our outrageously high lo-cal property taxes, our public school system employed a qualified instructor to give the sex talk for every parent in the district. I'd seen "health class" on his grade card, but it hadn't dawned on me that that was code for "sex ed," which was taught by one of the no-nonsense coaches, who was as subtle as a daisy cutter bomb.

One week the heath class instructor sent a note home that read: "Next week we'll be following our sexual education curriculum. Don't be shocked if your ninth grader brings up how to use a latex dam."

How dare they usurp my parental authority and responsibility? some parents probably thought, but my immediate reaction was what's a latex dam and what was the matter with the old-fashioned concrete kind?

Health class had done my dirty work, covering first, second, and third bases and sliding into home plate. Later I remembered that my son had gotten an A in health class; maybe he could answer a few questions for his father, who was officially off the hook sex ed–wise for the rest of his life because our two girls would be the responsibil-ity of my wife.

"What kind of birth control do you and Dad use, or are you in menopause?" My middle girl, Mary, asked my wife a litany of prickly questions each day after health class. Thankfully, when Peter took the class he never uttered a word about it, but his sister could not have been more different. Mary wanted her mother's take on family planning, organ function, and maintenance.

"My teacher says it's common for people to give their private parts nicknames. Do you and Dad have nicknames for your private parts?" An icy glare was her answer, and despite it being an inappropriate question to raise in front of her younger sister, she was not pun-ished, because our family had just outlawed waterboarding. Mean-while Sally, barely a teenager during that exchange, had no idea what Mary was talking about, but giggled because her sister said "private parts."

In the upcoming year, our youngest child will be enrolled in that infamous health class, where the coach indelicately explains the ins and outs of sex. Our first two children picked up their working knowledge of it that way, but in my heart I think it is still a parent's responsibility. That revelation came to me as I was driving Sally home from swim practice, when I announced a U-turn and pulled into our nearby Barnes & Noble, where, deep in the used-book bin, I found a thirty-five-year-old bestseller with a rubber tree on the cover.

"If you have any questions, ask Mom," I said, handing her the Time-Life classic. "If you need me, I'll be at the Yankee game."

16

Worry

Don't Fall Off That Volcano

My nine-year-old daughter had been gone thirty seconds too long, and I was pretending to listen to our tour guide but wondering what was taking so long. A landmark moment, it was the first time I'd ever let her go to the ladies' room on her own without me standing sentry in case there was screaming, so I could burst through the door for a rescue. But truthfully the only toilet sounds I've heard from my children are not the kind of noises you run toward.

A tug from behind, and Sally grabbed my hand and pulled me down close to her face to whisper, "Daddy, there was a weird old guy who talked to me in the bathroom."

Weird old guy in the bathroom?

A moment ago I was worried that she'd been abducted, had her hair dyed, and been shipped off to Venezuela to be sold into some child-slavery thing, but that was my automatic worst-case-scenario fear. This was a real problem, and I hadn't been there for my girl.

"He jiggled the doorknob, and as soon as I opened the door he barged in. Daddy, I was scared."

"Stay here," I said, pushing her into the immediate vicinity of her mother, and I quickly rounded the corner to stand next to the restroom so I could lasso the sicko who had startled my little girl. The only reason I'd allowed her to make the fifty-foot trip down the hall and around the corner was because we were in the most secure office building in the world. Inside I could hear the water running; in a moment he'd be out and I'd let him have it. I had waited for this moment twenty years guarding bathroom doors for my three kids. Standing vigil, I'd lost count of the number of odd looks I'd gotten from adult nonparents who wondered why that grown man was loitering outside the john. "Just waiting for Junior," I'd say, and point toward the door.

Sure, Perv Griffin.

Toilet sentinel is a father's job, and finally I had somebody who had done something that scared one of my children, and it was time for me to give him a piece of my limited mind. The doorknob turned and suddenly I was nose to nose with the scary bathroom barger-inner, Donald Rumsfeld.

"You're next," Rumsfeld said with a smile as he walked past me.

Shell-shocked and flash-frozen like Lot's wife, I stepped into the restroom, which was within fifty feet of the Oval Office. Rumsfeld was obviously heading into a meeting with his boss, the commander in chief, and wanted to make sure he could listen to an hour of Crawford talk without having to excuse himself to the boys' room. Moments earlier I had been prepared to lecture him on bathroom etiquette, but he was the secretary of defense, so if I yelled at him we might return home to find smoldering rubble and the tail fin from a cruise missile.

After flushing the West Wing toilet with my foot, I vowed that this would be the last White House tour our family took on a full bladder. As I walked back, a random thought entered my mind. I'd been in the bathroom after Sally before, and I wondered whether, when Rumsfeld went in there, he was greeted with what the Department of Defense might consider nerve gas.

"Sally, I saw the man you were talking about. Do you know who he is?" I asked. She shook her head. Then I followed up with the more delicate question of air quality. "After your visit are they going to have to retile?" That was our family's way of gauging how long to wait before another human should enter the facility in question.

She giggled. The British torched the White House once, so I was happy to hear Sally answer in the negative, because she was our one child who had the uncanny talent of turning a respectable restroom into a hazmat scene.

Mothers mother, fathers fret. I worry about my kids all the time. Will somebody bother them in the bathroom? Will they grow up happy? Will they make the team? Can I afford their college? Will they marry somebody who surfs the Net without pants?

My friend Jeisohn told me, "My father was soooooo worried when I was a teenager that I might be gay."

This was apparently a common worry of some fathers. Another acquaintance told me that when he came home with an earring, his father's body went limp. "You know, son, the only ones with earrings are gays and pirates," his father said. "So there better be a boat in the front yard."

Meanwhile Jeisohn's father worried that his son would grow up a homosexual. "He wanted to toughen me up, so he sent me for the summer to work on a trawler."

When he arrived dockside, the captain assessed his seaman skills and then assigned Jeisohn to breakfast duty, where he would operate the toaster, and when he wasn't lightly browning, he'd be tanning on the bow of the boat while the fishing was going on in the back.

His father wanted to get his son's thoughts off of men, yet he'd inadvertently marooned him in the Mediterranean on a small ship watching sweaty shirtless sailors flex and strain hours on end, dragging heaving nets of seafood onto the boat. It was perhaps the *last* place on earth his father should have sent him, considering Father's concerns. So did the summer toughen him up? Absolutely—he eventually became a logger in the Pacific Northwest and dressed in lumberjack shirts from the Bob the Builder collection.

Just kidding. He moved to New York City to be a hairdresser.

Worry is in the DNA of dads. It's a natural thought process that starts when the nurse makes the inky footprints of the baby, and doesn't end until they toe-tag the father.

I was driving somewhere one night when Harry Chapin's "Cat's in the Cradle" came on the radio, the song where the dad laments after his son has grown up that his boy never calls or visits because when he was young, his dad was too busy to play with him, and now the old man is alone.

Listening to Harry's sorry saga, I wondered whether I'd spent enough time with my son, because later that month he was moving to college. I had to make sure our last few days together would be something that he'd never forget.

"Peter, we're going to bike down a volcano!"

I knew when he heard "bike down a volcano" he envisioned the two of us on NASA-engineered carbon fiber mountain bikes wearing asbestos space suits careening down the side just as the volcano blows sky-high chunks of magma the size of Volkswagens.

Flying low over the Pacific on our final approach it was hard to miss Mount Haleakala—it makes up 75 percent of the island of Maui. The name Haleakala is Hawaiian for "house of the sun," but they should really call it "house of the early wake-up call" because to make sure that we were up at the top in time for sunrise, the bike tour company picked us up in a van at our hotel at one thirty in the morning. I had been sound asleep nine minutes before the annoyed hotel operator told us to get the hell up.

To wake up I sucked down a double espresso mega mocha venti Coolatta that my wife insisted I consume, so that I was completely coherent when I had the boy in my control, because our son was our financial future, and I wasn't supposed to let anything bad happen to him, because one day he would be a prosperous businessman who'd reward his parents with a luxury retirement villa in Provence, since they had sacrificed so much. I'd carried my lunch every day to work for thirty years, and his mother had bought off-the-rack Ann Taylor when she really wanted Prada. Nothing would happen on my watch to our future gravy train.

We arrived at the volcano bike base camp in the middle of the night, where thrill seekers were issued all manner of lifesaving safety equipment. We would be personally outfitted, as soon as we signed waivers that said if we were killed our heirs would not sue the bike company that had made our tragic deaths in paradise possible.

"You didn't designate a next of kin," the kid with the earring in his eyebrow reminded me as he pointed me to a blurry line on the living will and organ-donor form.

For the first time I realized that despite the glorious color photos on the Internet, there was an actual danger component to riding down a volcano; after all, when you ride the teacups at Disney World they don't first make you fill out a form giving away your spleen.

At approximately three thirty in the morning we had left the base camp and were approaching the entrance to the volcano road. We'd been in Maui for days and never actually seen the top of the mountain, because it was so incredibly high that there were always clouds surrounding the peak, which added to the mystery. In the dead of night the only thing you could see was whatever the headlights carved out straight ahead. I could not see how far down the cliffs went, so I figured the federal government surely would not let the general public mount a volcano unless it was completely safe, and I convinced myself that barely beyond my view were huge safety nets, just in case.

"Anybody ever go over the side?" I asked the driver.

Pointing dead ahead he said, "Actually, a couple from Germany missed that corner," and then he made a gesture with his hand flying straight away from his chest followed by a nose-diving gesture punctuated with a splat sound he made with his mouth that sounded like somebody just had gas, which woke up Peter.

"Don't worry, though," he assured us. "I haven't lost anybody since Tuesday." It was a Wednesday morning.

After a forty-five-minute climb up the volcano we pulled into the parking lot at the summit. Ten thousand twenty-three feet above sea level, and according to the dashboard thermometer it was thirty-five degrees outside.

"If I'm on a flaming volcano, why am I freezing?" inquired my son, who was probably expecting a molten crater of fire where the locals were about to throw a virgin into the abyss.

The doors to the vans were closed to keep the warm air in and the cold out, but after about fifteen minutes the smell of exhaust fumes was so thick, I could feel my brain stem throbbing, and I worried that when it was time to bike down, I'd be so high I'd say, "Time to fly . . . ," and forget to take that left turn like the German tourists and wind up in the big schnitzel stand in the sky.

"Let's get some fresh air," I said to my son, who would have preferred to lose a few million brain cells stewing in the warm truck fumes, rather than traipse around a volcano top with his old man. "Watch your step out there," the guide told us. "We had a guy fall off the face in April. . . . They only found his shoes."

The summit in the pitch black was as dark a place as I'd ever been in my life, a fact not lost on the federal government. Years earlier Uncle Sam's scientists had calculated that because this volcano summit was located above one-third of the atmosphere, and the air was clear and dry and still, and there was virtually no light reflection from major cities, this was the best place on the planet to see things at night, so they'd hauled in the world's strongest telescopes and pointed them mostly at the stars, although supposedly one was constantly trained on a Honolulu high-rise popular with Swedish flight attendants.

Not only was it dark, it was dead quiet, the kind of scary silence in movies just before the *T. rex* leans out from behind the palm tree and eats the cave girl.

We huddled for an hour, until an eerie glow grew in the east; then we moved toward the volcano rim, waiting for the official sunrise. One hundred and seventy-five tourists marveled at the most magnificent daybreak on earth staring directly at the solar fireball. Many probably took that moment to contemplate their place in the universe; I simply wondered what permanent damage I was doing to my retinas. Exhausted yet exhilarated, I stared directly at the solar fireball like a beagle reading the *New York Post*. To celebrate future glaucoma and the long-awaited sun, the tourists spontaneously burst into applause.

"What'd ya think?" I asked my son.

Standing on the crater's edge bathed in a glorious golden glow far above the Pacific was as profound an experience as any I'd had in my lifetime.

"It's nice. Can we eat?"

Above the clouds, two miles in the sky, our fast-food choices were somewhat limited.

"At the first Taco Bell, we'll do the drive-through," I promised, knowing that would be as likely as finding a bookish intellectual at a monster truck pull.

The first three packs of bike riders had started their downhill trips and we were next, so we started queuing up on our state-of-the-art volcano-riding bikes. As I screwed on my safety helmet, I came to the scary realization that the three shots of espresso with a plain coffee chaser, combined with having sucked down the exhaust of idling buses for an hour and a half, had made me absolutely dizzy. I might describe it as feeling "high," but I might one day run for elected office, and I'd hate to have this come back to haunt me, so "dizzy" is as far as my campaign strategists will allow me to go.

I added my occasional vertigo to the equation and was confident that sometime in the next ten minutes a man with a stethoscope would be loading me on a medevac helicopter for the trip to some nearby tropical hospital, where a nurse in a muumuu would ask the doctor how he intended to remove the macadamia nut tree from my large-intestine area.

Initially I thought somebody at the top would yell, "Let's ride!" and we'd take off like a chuck wagon race, but because the paved road was only one lane in each direction, we would have to bike down single file. We gathered in a semicircle while our guide gave final instructions and made riding assignments. My son was the youngest rider and wound up with the pole position; I'm sure our guide thought my boy was good at bicycling, but in reality the longest ride he'd ever made was from our house to the Dairy Queen, and we'd gotten so winded, we'd pushed our bikes uphill, and the Dilly Bars had wound up a puddle of chocolate goo.

"Chief," the tour guide addressed me, "you're riding last."

Perfect. That was the safest slot, I figured, and if bicyclists started careening off the road, I would safely brake to a stop and wave hysterically to an orbiting NSA satellite to stop intercepting Michael Moore's cell phone calls and send an ambulance.

"Because we're on a schedule we're going to have to average seventeen miles an hour," the guide told us. "Everybody okay with that speed?" We all nodded our approval, except for a hesitant woman from Cleveland who'd ridden up the mountain next to me in the van. "I can't do that, that's too fast for me," she said.

Why didn't they mention the seventeen-mile-an-hour mandate at the base camp or in the brochure? I wondered as the woman climbed into the chase vehicle, which had carted our bikes up to the top. Later I would learn that the woman was actually hard of hearing, and thought the leader said we had to average *seventy* miles an hour.

"Let's go!" the bike wrangler hollered, and my son led the way. As we started down it finally dawned on me what was so weird—it was my first bike ride *above* the clouds, where airplanes belonged. It was surreal, especially given my rusty bike skills, gas-fume delirium, and profound fear of volcanoes. Two minutes into the ride I made my first big turn and looked to the right only to notice that I was on a narrow ledge of asphalt atop a three-thousand-foot drop to certain death. Could somebody please remind me why I was here and not at the pool drinking a mojito?

We didn't have to pedal to go fast—the decline was so substantial that gravity did all the work, and the longer you went without using your brake, the faster you'd roll. I discovered that the hard way when I momentarily lost track of my paranoia and realized I was freewheeling about thirty-five miles an hour on a road that looked like it was a BMW test track. I was going way too fast for someone who last rode a bike thirty years earlier on Sunday mornings throwing the *Kansas City Times* into my neighbors' bushes. Impulsively I grabbed the hand brake and kept a constant pressure on it, slowing down to the approximate speed of those motorized carts the elderly use at the mall.

Riding the brake seemed like a nice alternative to zooming off the side until I nonchalantly turned around and realized that three feet behind me was the chase truck. My safety helmet had kept me from hearing its engine, and suddenly I realized that if I didn't fly off the volcano I would fall and get cow-catchered by the grill of a Ford Econovan.

At our water break the bike leader approached me. "You okay, chief?"

"Doing great!" I smiled back, when in fact I'd rather have driven upholstery nails into my shins.

"You've got to speed up or we're going to miss lunch."

I was on vacation and yet some guy with a hula girl tattoo on his neck *whom I was paying a lot of money to* said hurry it up. The nerve. Then I looked over and my son was giving me a "You okay, Dad?" glance.

"I've just been sightseeing. I'll go faster because I'd hate to miss a lunch I've already paid for!"

We made it to lunch on time. In fact, I went so fast for the final ten miles that I was neck and neck with my son at the front of the pack—we were having our own personal Tour de France. I felt like Lance Armstrong, except for the Sheryl-Crow-was-once-my-girlfriend part.

We stopped at the Road to Hana at the edge of the Pacific to take a picture of two guys having one of their five best days ever. That day we saw the sun rise above the clouds, we traveled down a volcano, and we didn't die.

After that guy told me to speed up, I did, even though it was high and it was scary and there was a chance that one of us might get hurt. But standing there I realized that at that moment, life was as perfect as it gets. It was me and my boy slaying the volcano.

The only fear I had left came from knowing that our great day would not last forever, because the good stuff never does.

Then I thought practically for a moment and recognized that even if I rode off the side of that two-mile-high lawsuit, I would die in paradise. And if I went *Thelma and Louise* over the side of that volcano, I would easily be the lead story on the Fox News Channel for most of one or maybe two complete news cycles, and I might even get a chopper over my funeral procession, unless Britney Spears was getting a car wash at the same time.

Booze

From Tang to Tanqueray

My wife, Kathy, wiped a tear from the corner of her eye as she gazed at our daughter standing there in her imported Italian white lace gown and a flowing veil that cascaded down past her shoulders. I had a lump in my throat knowing what a big day this was and how things would change after she walked down the aisle. As the father I took my place next to my teary wife as Sally stood at the front of the church with a young man we barely knew. But that was okay—it wasn't as if she was going to marry the guy. It was her first Holy Communion and she was seven.

My practical yet very fashion-forward wife had purchased the aforementioned dress that week at Daffy's, where their slogan is "Clothing Bargains for Millionaires." The clerk who sold it to her knew we weren't millionaires—my wife had a coupon.

Sally was not the only girl in what looked like a girl's size 6 wedding dress. They all wore one because first Communion was a big deal in our town outside New York. It was a Catholic version of a bar mitzvah, without the chocolate fountain.

"Like a shepherd . . . ," the choir sang as my girl led her classmates up to the monsignor, who lifted a host squarely in front of her face. "Body of Christ," he announced.

We had joked earlier that because she had always been the family rebel with a devil streak, the instant she got her first Communion, the church would be hit by a lightning bolt, or an IRS audit.

"Amen," she said, crossing herself.

She turned toward us in the first row, and I gave her a little thumbs-up signal to let her know how proud we were. That was when we realized she wasn't returning to her seat. Instead, she kept walking toward the Eucharistic minister holding up the gold chalice filled with sacramental wine, which seemed a little adult for second graders, but because our church didn't ask for a photo ID there was no stopping her.

Barely four feet tall, hands folded together in prayer she gave the minister a nod that a bartender might mistake for the *hit me* look. A symbolic tiny taste is all one is to take, but to me it looked like she was chugging it.

"Amen," she said, returning the chalice after becoming the first member of our hypochondriacal family ever to drink the Communion wine during the cold and flu season.

Sally had been first in line, and the priest had told everybody to follow her, so when she ad-libbed and went for the rosé, everybody followed in her revolutionary footsteps. After her holy swig heard round the parish, she turned and gave us a little *mmm-tasty* smirk and then led her second-grade classmates back to their pew.

My wife and I were shell-shocked; she'd never had any form of alcohol before—we had been absolutely vigilant about booze, even though other parents were much less restrictive. I was at a backyard party where one father was laughing it up about how the previous Friday night as he was presiding over the family bar he'd built in the basement he asked his fourteen-year-old son, "What'll it be, Frankie?"

The boy, who at that moment was wearing a *SpongeBob Square-Pants* T-shirt, had a very un-Nickelodeon answer: "Dad, gimme a Jack 'n' Coke, twist of lime."

Does that sound like the first drink a young man would order? Shouldn't it be a beer or Cold Duck? And who before the age of twenty has ever ordered anything *with a twist of lime,* other than George Clooney? My gut told me that was not his first drink nor even his second, and that kid would be blowing a Breathalyzer number into the turpentine zone by the time he was shaving.

One night we went out for a meal at a local Italian restaurant and spotted a neighborhood father having dinner in a corner booth with his son. The mother and daughters were out of town, and it was a guys' night out. It was a bring-your-own-bottle establishment, and after the waiter uncorked a bottle of red wine, he first poured the father a glass and then filled a full tumbler for the seventeen-year-old son, in our state where the drinking age was twenty-one. If the dad let the kid drink openly in public, what was he doing at home, Jell-O shots off the dinette set?

Kathy and I were horrified, but then again we were raising our children in a zero-tolerance household. "This fruitcake has real rum in it!" My son giggled, taking another big bite.

Wasn't fruitcake how Joplin got hooked? Isn't it a gateway baked good? First they buy some online at www.boozyfruitcake.com, then they're skipping school to score some on the street, and next thing you know they're drinking Benadryl from a boot. My parents never served fruitcake, not because it was an intoxicant, but because it had the consistency of cat litter.

My wife and I'd heard horror stories from various deans of admissions who said that when kids made the transition to college life, if they'd had a taste in high school, being around the stuff in college was no big deal, but once those like my son, Peter, who'd lived a monastic high school life, got to college, they went crazy, and by noon the second day their clothes would stink of Colt 45 and there was a better than average chance that the night before they did something stupid that they'd not remember until the DVD release of *Freshman Without Pants*.

With less than a week before Peter started college, I worried about his transition from Ovaltine to high octane. He would promise not to touch the stuff, but once he arrived in his ivory tower the peer pressure of a cute premed student in a belly shirt with a funnel would surely short-circuit his—any young man's—common sense. That's when I made the decision that I would be there for his first drink, just to make sure nothing happened. But I couldn't follow him around campus, because that would make him look like a daddy's boy, and the last thing he needed was for his new friends to think that he was our poodle.

This brainstorm or alcohol epiphany occurred halfway through our final vacation of the year, which would end in three days with him going to college. The last thing I wanted my daughters to see was their father plying their brother with moonshine, so I got somebody else to do my dirty work—the Walt Disney Company.

Four days earlier when we checked into the resort I saw a very famous entertainment TV reporter in the lobby, who asked me if I was there for the junket. When I told him that we were simply on vacation he revealed that Disney television was flying in reporters from across the country for a party to mark the DVD release of the show *Lost*. Being a world-class gate-crasher, I twisted some arms, and being a media member, I got my son and me invited. It was past eleven that night when we arrived, the party was deep in a jungle and featured a huge plywood cutout of the *Lost* crew's crashed plane with smoke billowing out of engine number two. Amid the chaos was exactly what you'd expect to see next to the wreckage of an airliner that just ditched in the Pacific, go-go dancing flight attendants.

"What'll it be?" the bartender asked as we both looked at the thematic drink menu. Earlier I had told Peter that I wanted him to have his first taste of firewater in front of me and that he should choose any drink he wanted.

"I'll have the *Lost* Luggage," my son said, and I squinted to read that that was a cute name for Red Bull and vodka. Thank goodness he didn't ask for a Jack 'n' Coke, twist of lime; if he had I would have immediately placed him under hut arrest. I knew he ordered it only because he'd never had a Red Bull, and because it was already 11 P.M., I told him to pick another.

"You pick," he told me, which was my chance to regulate his alcohol intake.

"He'll have the Plane Crash Cosmo."

Not quite twenty-one, he was not of legal drinking age; however, at six feet four inches tall, he was certainly of legal drinking height.

"There you go, guys," the barkeep said, sliding two drinks in our direction. To be honest, after years of standing on my soapbox, reminding my children of the evils of alcohol, it felt downright surreal that I was standing under a banyan tree two miles from where my wife at that moment was in our room watching the second rerun of *The O'Reilly Factor* as our only son sucked down an honest-to-goodness top-shelf cocktail.

"Whatdaya think?"

"It's good" was all he said after he inhaled it in a single slurp. He had obviously never had clear alcohol before, because nobody aside from a guy with a blindfold on a firing line could down something that toxic, that fast.

He put down his empty martini glass as I nursed mine, and we went to chat up the stars of the show, which I had never seen before. By the way, Matthew Fox was a very nice guy. An hour later I insisted that Peter have another drink, and he did.

Slurp.

At last call, before they closed the rain forest, he had one final aperitif. I'd wanted him to get a taste of alcohol before he went to college, and I'd accomplished that goal; however, after three very strong drinks I realized there was one tiny problem with my 160-pound baby—he was still shockingly sober.

I thought by now he'd be bent over behind the ukulele stand puking his guts out, getting a taste of the aftereffects of cocktailing; instead, he seemed absolutely fine. Had he developed an alcohol resistance after drinking all through high school, and we never caught on, because he wasn't slurring his words, not bobbing or weaving? In the hall outside our rooms, I made a tactical decision right then that we would not be discussing my little social-engineering experience with my wife, his mother.

"Let's keep this our little secret." He nodded, and we closed the door on my misguided night out with the boy.

The next morning around nine as we were leaving for our all-you-can-eat breakfast buffet my wife announced reveille, and within a few minutes Mary and Sally appeared, smoothing their hair down atop their heads.

"Where is Peter?" my wife inquired. When told he was still in bed, my wife walked to their door and demanded, "Peter, we're going, get up."

"I'll be right there," he groaned in a voice that was slow and raspy.

"We're going down to breakfast. Meet us there," she said, and then turned to me. "I think he got too much sun."

If she only knew.

Half an hour later, Peter dragged his carcass to the breakfast table; the whites of his eyes were the same color red as a Campbell's soup can. At that moment he needed to soak his entire face in Visine.

"Can I get you a plate for the buffet?" the waiter asked.

"No . . . thank . . . you," he mumbled while shielding his squinty eyes as if somebody were arc-welding at the table.

As my wife worried that he'd gotten too much sun, I sat there basking in the glory of my experiment, because my son had not only tried his first cocktail, but got a deluxe taste of Hangover City, all while supervised by his father, who'd been there just in case. As for my wife of twenty-something years, because I'd plied with a bevy of beverages one of the children she'd kept tightly under her wing every day of their lives, I did not tell her what I'd done for one calendar year, when the official statute of limitations on stupid ran out.

If you're shocked at my methods, don't be. When I was a teenager I was legally drinking at eighteen because back then it was the drinking age. If I did it, why couldn't he? Ultimately that one-night experiment was a success that changed his life. He told me three years later he'd never again had so much as a sip of clear alcohol since that night, because he'd seen what trouble it could lead to. Mission accomplished.

While I personally indoctrinated my son, I don't think I'll have to do the same with my youngest. After her Holy Communion sip she went to a party at a friend's home, and while running willy-nilly inside a rented Moon Bounce, she abruptly ripped her brand-new Italian embroidered Communion gown from Daffy's.

"My mom's going to be mad. Could you say you did it?" she asked the hostess, who informed her that she certainly would not.

Realizing her rambunctiousness could have been the direct result of losing control while under the influence, Sally made a vow that day that she would never drink wine again, because of what it did to her, and because it tasted like medicine. She hated medicine. We were also lucky our church used value-priced wine in a box; she might have gone Drew Barrymore if our parish could afford something that came with a cork.

18

Role Reversal

The Parent Trapped

Mary and Sally," I addressed my high school girls as I served up a couple short stacks of flapjacks, "if we could do anything today, what would it be?"

"Let's get manicures!"

That was not the answer I was expecting. It was like discovering that Lou Dobbs was an illegal alien.

"Mommy takes us all the time. Puh-lease?"

Welcome to New Jersey, the nail salon state, with the highest per capita consumption of acetone in the civilized world. Allow me to explain how seriously women in the Garden State take their nails. A lovely mother of two had just gotten her nails done. She didn't want to smear her still-tacky fingers on the seat belt, so she decided not to buckle it for her five-block trip home. While she was waiting at a stoplight, a teenager blew the light, sending her through the windshield.

"She didn't feel a thing," her best friend told me at her funeral. "This is how she'd want to go. Look at her nails—they're *perfect*."

That's how powerful the pull to polish is where I live, so if my girls wanted to go out for manicures while Mom was busy, I could certainly drive them over; they surely had a three-year-old *Popular Mechanics* magazine in the spot wherever the menfolk waited for their beautified women.

As I was pulling into a spot at the strip mall, Mary got me a second time. "What are you getting, Dad?"

Whoa, hold it right there, Shorty. That was not part of the deal. I had no intention of getting a treatment of any sort at that clip joint. I was just their chauffeur, who'd pay at the end.

"Come on, Dad!" They were giving me the same look our golden retriever gives me to open the sliding door so he can come inside and drag his dog butt across our living room rug.

Doing an instant damage assessment, I didn't spot any cars I recognized in the lot. The salon was five doors down from Starbucks, so chances were none of my regular coffee swillers would see me. So I took a gamble. Keep in mind I had never had anything like this done before and thought the whole lotion and potion thing on guys was weird, although I did once laugh at something on *Will and Grace*.

"Okay, what would you suggest for a gentleman, ladies?"

Their answer was unanimous, a mani-pedi, which is salon slang for getting a manicure and pedicure; I explain that for any Montana or Wyoming cowboys reading this by campfire light.

"Do you have the punch card?" Mary asked Sally as we entered the reception area; my wife had a card that was just one punch away from a free visit, because every tenth visit you could have any single body part trimmed or tweezed for free. Leonid Brezhnev, the authoritarian leader of Russia with the big Brooke Shields bushy monobrow, would have loved this place.

My girls were regulars, and as soon as the door opened, the woman in charge greeted them by name and asked what they'd like done. I immediately took charge as the alpha dad.

"A manicure for Sally, with a palm tree."

"Very nice." She nodded her approval. "Last time she had a beach ball."

"And Mary will have the manicure *and* pedicure," I said in the loud voice so that nearby customers would hear that Mr. Big Spender was splurging for both, the nail equivalent of surf and turf.

Then I dropped the bomb. "And I'd like a manicure and spa pedicure as well."

Four or five matrons swiveled their heads around, Linda Blair–style, to see the man who wanted his toes painted.

"You do serve guys, don't you?"

"Of course," she said as I imagined she nervously depressed a hidden button with her foot that would warn the luxuriating ladies there was a man in the house.

"Penny!" The receptionist summoned a sturdy young woman who looked Korean but insisted she was from South America, who was apparently on staff to handle the more complicated cuticle cases, like split toenails or men.

As I walked back, every single woman paused for a moment to look up from her *Vogue* or *Better Homes and Gardens.* They stared at me mouths agape as if I had last year's haircut.

I was directed to a burgundy leather massage chair much like the one Sharper Image has in its window, except instead of a footstool this one had a five-gallon foot tub. Once I was barefoot, Penny gritted her teeth and took a good look at the science project I'd been growing for the better part of forty-five years. Surely the last time she'd seen feet like mine was in *Shrek.*

Without a word she gave my feet an extra squirt of some sort of something that burned on contact. I tried to sneak a glance to see if it was an insecticide from the Black Flag family.

"They must be for a man—they're called man-icures!" I cracked, trying to break the spa ice.

(Crickets.)

Sally was having second thoughts about my being on the premises. While I didn't know anybody there, she did: cheerleaders from her high school, the dip-cone girl from Dairy Queen, and half a dozen vaguely familiar women from church who'd apparently heard a man was coming in and wanted a good seat. Meanwhile my older daughter, Mary, sat smiling her approval of my doing something so evolved. "Dad, you're so Clay Aiken."

A word about a pedicure—it does not feel good. After the burning squirt bottle, Penny got out what I would gauge from my wood shop days was a 60-grit sandpaper stick, and sanded off things. Once satisfied, she picked up a razor-sharp stainless-steel contraption that looked like one of those vegetable slicers advertised on late-night television and whacked off more years of dangling skin parts. It was absolute torture. Why were these nail salon girls working in New Jersey and not Gitmo, where they would have those terrorists singing like canaries?

Not wanting to appear a wussy, I said nothing about the pain and instead observed the half a cup of dry dead skin debris she'd just harvested from my feet. "Penny, good job making the grated Parmesan."

"Thank you, Mr. Steve. Now I never eat pizza again."

"Way to go, Dad," whispered Sally.

"Your father is very liberated," the woman next to Mary told her as Mary sent a text message to her mother that read exactly: "its fun 2 c dad interact w/the staff."

Ten minutes later my wife got another text that read: "Dad's eyes are closed. He doesn't know it, but they're putting polish on his toenails! Don't worry, it's clear, but very shiny!"

They didn't ask me about polish. Penny just pulled out the little bottle and slathered it over all ten of my little piggies. Please don't quote me on this, but they looked great. But my self-admiration was short-lived, as Penny directed her attention to my calves and kneecaps with a vigorous rubdown. I felt a little self-conscious with a total stranger massaging me in front of my children, but the kids nonchalantly watched the woman giving me the calf job. Why weren't they a teensy bit freaked out? It was like seeing your dad take a spin class with Elton John.

"Let's go," Penny announced as she pulled me up and escorted me toward the front of the store for my paraffin manicure.

"Hi, girls," I said to a trio of high school cheerleaders who giggled as they watched me waddle their way wearing a pair of paper flip-flops.

"My dad will get a manicure," the cheerleader from the middle of the pyramid said, "the instant a pig flies out of his butt."

The brunette tagged on a "My pops is clueless about what happens here. He doesn't even know what a Brazilian is," and they all burst into laughter.

"What's a Brazilian?" I discreetly whispered to Penny, who handed me a brochure explaining that a Brazilian was not only a person from Brazil, but also a painful waxing process performed by technicians who had made such poor career choices that they were paid to apply hot wax to total strangers' most private nooks and crannies and then briskly rip it out, making the recipients rue the day they started growing hair in those southern spots.

For my manicure Penny used nail clippers, which was much different from how I did my own nails, which was with a pair of scissors from Staples. By this time my daughters were hovering, watching Penny's precision much like medical students gathered around a famous cardiologist during a triple bypass. I just sat there and smiled; this was why we came: a father spending quality time with his girls. Then I realized they just wanted tip money.

"Back pocket," and they pulled out my wad of ones and looked for their manicurists and pedicurists. A few minutes later the work was completed on my hands and feet, and on my thirty-eight-dollar bill I tipped Penny ten bucks because of all the extra time involved, and because it was gross. This wasn't just a gratuity, it was hush money.

"Penny, ten dollars says I was never here." She happily slipped it into her apron as she returned to vacuuming up my piles of DNA with a Shop-Vac.

On the way out the door I spotted one of our annoying neighbors, whom we don't speak to because she dropped a dime on me to report the building of a tree house without a permit. As we passed her I turned to my daughters, and asked, "Did you enjoy your treatments, girls?"

"Yes, Daddy," Sally said.

"Me too! I think I'll get *another* Brazilian next week!" And just to add to the effect, I exited a bit bowlegged, much like my many Montana cowboy readers.

The father-daughter thing had worked out; I had shown them I wanted to be with them and was willing to leave my comfort zone and try something from their girly world. In turn they asked if I would take them into my 'hood.

"Can I go with you to the gym, Daddy?"

I loved showing Mary how all of the weight-lifting machines worked. She did the heavy lifting as I stood next to her and counted, from one to ten, over and over. She then ran on the treadmill much faster and farther than I could run as I marveled at how she was able to sweat like one was supposed to. Over the years I had developed what I called a "placebo workout," where my routine consisted of changing into my workout costume, stretching, chatting with friends, traversing from machine to machine doing a few non-life-threatening lifts, and finally taking off my workout costume, which, thanks to my sweat-free workout, was never soiled.

After our workouts Mary and I were headed to our separate changing rooms, and I had the satisfying feeling that I'd shown her the ropes of my old-man gym.

"You're lucky she wants to spend time with you. My girl's already married," a guy who always seemed to be at the gym when I worked out said from the other end of the locker room bench I was seated upon.

"We're lucky men to have girls who love us," I said.

I was expecting some sort of a response, but he said nothing. Perhaps he was struck by the shockingly profound conversation for two men in towels, or it could have been the telltale sign that I was not the man he'd thought I was.

"Hey, Steve," he said with his eyes cast downward, "what the hell happened to your toes? They're shiny. . . ."

19

Letting Go

I Can't Cut the Cord

y lone son and I arrived at Newark airport around eight on
the evening of July 4. Most of America at that moment had
already applied mosquito repellent and was seated in uncomfortable folding chairs that seem to be used but once a year as
our nation collectively commemorated our national anniversary the
way our forefathers intended, by blowing things up and frightening
wildlife.

Explosions were in fact all I could think of. It was two summers
after September 11, and despite the fun our high school sophomore
would soon be having with his cousin that summer at Oxford, the
fear was palpable in letting him fly alone thousands of miles across
an ocean filled with water and sharks and scary plankton that can
consume human flesh, all in the dead of the night. His mother was
too upset to go. We both put on brave faces, but I could tell he was
just as nervous as I.

"Anything you want to tell me before I go?" my seventeen-year-old
globe-trotter asked at the departure gate.

I paused for a moment. "Yes, there is. If you see a nice girl you'd
like to chat with, don't start with 'Are you allergic to duct tape?'"

A laugh, a hug, and he was gone.

The night he flew across the Atlantic was the first time he had
ever been away from home. Long after everyone had gone to bed, I

walked to his bedroom door and caught a whiff of the very essence of him, dirty tube socks and Axe body spray.

If he had been there, what would he have been looking at right then, other than *SportsCenter*? I lay on his bed. Directly overhead were the glow-in-the-dark stars we'd glued to his ceiling as a second-grade science project. They'd watched over him for most of his life. On that night, he was under the real stars, on his own.

The next night I returned to his room before going to bed to think about him, and the next night and the next, but I stopped before a full week had passed, because I was getting used to the idea that he was gone. At summer's end, we flew to London and took the train north to watch our boy clad in prep school blazer and khakis take part in a very spirited debate on something that made no sense to us.

Still our little boy, he seemed more worldly as he gave us his tour of Oxford University. His sisters were particularly impressed with the long dark dining hall where they filmed the Harry Potter movies. I made Sally put back the souvenir fork she tried to pinch from the table that sat under the levitating candles.

"Dad, don't walk there," he barked out as I strolled across the gorgeous lawn at Pembroke College.

"Peter, you're not the boss of me," I said proudly, co-opting a line from the *Malcolm in the Middle* theme song.

"It's against the rules," he insisted.

What happened to my calm son? He goes away to England and turns into Dick Cheney?

"Peter," I shot back, "you're telling me they have rules against walking on the grass?"

"Dad, it's not just grass, it's a graveyard."

Oh.

"A lot of the teachers who lived in these buildings," he said, pointing to the surrounding halls, "are buried in this courtyard."

My initial repulsion turned to a weird admiration of the lush green carpet, which was on a par with a fine golf course. At home I could fertilize only with Turf Builder; here they used English professors.

Walking with him as he gave us a guided tour, I was struck by how independent he seemed. I was very proud of my boy.

Four years later and it was my daughter Mary's turn to go to Oxford, and while I certainly trusted her as much as I did her brother, she was a girl, and I worried that with her wandering around England for the summer it would simply be a matter of time before she'd catch Prince William's eye, and by the end of her summer Mary's name would be on a terminal at Heathrow and I would get a cushy job as a viscount.

But before a prince offered her a glass slipper she would have to get to England, and there was a problem with that—the day she was to leave, a series of car bombs were found in London, and just as we were loading our SUV for the airport, my wife called me back into the house to watch a report from Sky News that a terrorist had rammed his bomb-laden Jeep Cherokee into the front door of the Glasgow airport and then lit the both of them on fire.

"The red zone is for loading and unloading car bombs. . . ."

Coincidentally, the last trip we'd planned had been for Mary's sweet sixteenth birthday, and rather than an extravagant party with scads of marginal friends and excessive decorating, she'd asked her mother to take her and her sister on a trip to Paris. Airline tickets were purchased, hotels were booked, and on the day they were to leave, hundreds of young Parisians decided to welcome Mary by lighting the suburbs on fire. Looting, violence, general chaos. Panicked that they'd be caught in the bedlam, my worried wife called Continental Airlines and spoke to a sympathetic reservation agent/ mother who agreed with my wife that the only thing that should be torched on a sweet sixteen was birthday candles and not a warehouse district. Au revoir, City of Frights.

Instead they flew west to southern California. They stayed at Shutters on the Beach in Santa Monica, where they worked out next to Jude Law in the fitness center and saw Pamela Anderson changing in the locker room.

"Dad," my youngest daughter, Sally, confessed later, "when I realized who that lady was who was undressing, I just thought one thing."

"Yes?" I said, knowing that the one thing she would think would be different from the one thing that came to my mind.

"Where's my camera phone? Do you know what the tabs would pay for that?"

Sally was one candid away from a full ride to college thanks to the *National Enquirer*. But there would be many more famous seminude celebrities for her to befriend. At that moment we were about to ship off her sister, Mary, to Oxford to study British history. But unlike her last aborted trip to Europe, this time it wasn't Molotov cocktails thrown by French teenagers who wanted jobs; the UK airport terminal attack was international terrorism.

"If she doesn't go, it means we've surrendered and the terrorists win," I told my wife, honestly believing that, kind of.

Terrorism is always easier to talk about when it affects other people, not a blood relative. At that point Mary had been in her room and not near a television, so she had still not seen or heard about the UK attack or the worldwide increase in the terror threat. Why should we tell her? It would only scare her. As she packed, my wife and I decided that because of the heightened state of alert, Heathrow was at that moment probably the safest airport in the world. The decision was made—she would go.

But we didn't know whether to tell her about the incident on the way to the airport or to just let her discover it on her own once she got there. She must have known something was up preflight because her brother and sister uncharacteristically burst into tears when they said good-bye, and all of our friends made urgent phone calls—"Are you going to let her go?"—which led to private conversations behind closed doors so that somebody who might be flying that day would not get as freaked out as her parents.

As we drove to the airport we did not listen to news radio because we didn't want her to hear one of the news bulletins. Instead we listened to Dr. Laura tell some woman who was stuck in a dead-end marriage to leave the womanizing bum to whom she was hitched.

"This is the hill you want to die on?" Dr. Laura lectured some call-in loser on XM.

I didn't want to think about hills or dying so I changed the channel and we listened to some guy in a monotone tell us that we should liquidate our 401(k) and invest in pork bellies.

At the gate Mary, who by that time knew about the terrorist attack, was a picture of maturity. When it was time to say good-bye, she put on her brave face and then walked through security backward so she could see us every step of the way until a partition got in our way, and she was gone. I was trusting the guys with the Uzis would keep her safe between our house and the land of Quidditch.

Wondering whether we'd made the right decision to send her, my wife and I spoke not a word on the way home, instead listening to the news on the radio of the attack, and how they'd gotten some leads and were about to launch a series of raids to head off another attack. I had an uneasy feeling about letting her go. It was the right thing for her . . . wasn't it? When my wife and I got home, I went to the airline website and punched in her flight number. As I waited for that screen to load on that day of international airport terror, I was instantly scared to death.

Call the airline.

That was the same online notation for the planes that crashed on 9/11. I dialed her cell phone, and got nothing, not even her voice mail message. I found another flight tracker, identical message.

Call the airline.

Why couldn't she have gone to summer camp in the Berkshires, where the only worry was about flies the size of canned hams? I picked up the cordless and dialed the 800 number for the airline.

"Due to an unusually high call volume, your call will be answered by the next operator in approximately twenty-three minutes."

Twenty-three minutes? Why was the airline switchboard suddenly jammed at nine o'clock on a Sunday? *BECAUSE SOMETHING BAD WAS HAPPENING, AND I WASN'T THERE TO PROTECT MY DAUGHTER!*

Tempted to hang up and call another number, I knew I'd just lose my place in line, so with speakerphone on, I went fishing on the Web, where panicked parents can become hyperspeed typists. Five other flight trackers all issued the same disturbing notation, but after I was eighteen minutes on hold, I was back at her airline site and got a suddenly different notation: *Taxiing for takeoff.*

What changed from *Call the Airline* to *Taxiing for takeoff*? It didn't matter. I sat at the computer clicking—REFRESH—every fifteen seconds, as it gave me a virtual real-time status report; *Taxiing for takeoff. Altitude, 0 feet. Altitude, 0 feet. Altitude,0 feet. Altitude, 50 feet.* I held my breath, watching to make sure the numbers went up and not down. *Altitude, 120 feet.* I continued until her flight was cruising 35,000 feet away from anything the plane could run into, like buildings, mountains, or icebergs.

At bedtime I replayed the ritual of going to her room and sitting on her bed, but this time I didn't feel sad; I felt very alone. This was what it would be like when she and her brother and her little sister all moved away. It would be painfully quiet. I sat there and wondered if she was frightened, or if she even knew what was happening on the ground in the United Kingdom. I stared at a third-grade Halloween costume photograph of Mary dressed as Mary Queen of Hearts. Things used to be so simple.

As dads we try not to show when we're scared or worried, but truth be told, the most frightening times are when we have no control over what's happening. When the kids are somewhere we can't see them, or talk to them, or squeeze them, we have to hope and pray that they are safe, and that if something comes up, they'll be wise enough to improvise. Twelve hours after *Call the airline,* our phone rang.

"Hi, Dad!"

"Hi, Mary. You took off late. . . ."

"We did? Didn't notice. Daddy, it's real pretty here today," and she launched into an excited recitation of who she'd met and where she'd been and how she'd momentarily lost her bag. "I just met the nicest boy. His name is Eduardo, and he taught me how to salsa dance!" I could hear kids laughing in the background; I felt a wave of relief wash over me until the cell phone abruptly cut off.

"Hello . . . Mary . . . Hello?"

I waited a minute for her to call back, but nothing, so I dialed her cell phone. It rang and rang and rang some more. Where was she? Was she with Eduardo? Wait a minute, who was Eduardo the salsa dancer? What was the legal age for marriage without parental consent in that country? As I Googled an answer I reminded myself of one of my wife's sayings, *Paranoia will destroy ya,* which was true, but as her father it was natural for me to imagine the worst possible scenario was unfolding at some undisclosed location, in another country. I hit redial again, and a man answered. It was not Eduardo.

"Hi, this is Chuck Norris. . . ."

For her sixteenth birthday I had asked *the real* Chuck Norris—the same guy about whom somebody on the Internet has invented hundreds of Chuck Norris-isms, like "Chuck Norris has two speeds, walk and kill," the Mr. Norris who was one of Mary's cultural icons—to record her phone message. He had graciously complied, and his message was what I was hearing.

"Mary Doocy can't come to the phone right now, because we're out fighting crime," Chuck Norris announced in his famous monotone. "Leave your message at the sound of the snapping neck." *Beeeeeeeep.*

"Mary, it's Dad. Call us when you can."

It was hard for me to let my son travel alone to England, but it was exponentially tougher for a father to let his little princess fly away from our little cocoon to the land of the kidney pie. For every parent saying good-bye to any children, regardless of the time apart, it is tough. We raise them as best we can, we teach them stuff like how to start a pilot light or change the spare tire, even though we know they're not paying attention, because they know we'll always be there to help them. And just when our children get to be young adults and truly a joy to be around, they leave us to start their own lives.

Mary would return in five weeks, and we would all survive what was her first big step toward a lifetime of independence. She knows that wherever she goes and whatever she does, between her mother, her siblings, Chuck Norris, and me, she'll never be alone.

20

College

Can I Pay with Bonus Miles?

The University of San Diego is a stunning movie-set campus atop a mountain. My daughter Mary was very interested in attending, and I could see why. Some campuses have tanning pools; others, sushi bars. This one had both, and an In 'N' Out Burger down the hill. After a ninety-minute tour, we walked through one of the dorms, which had an impressive security system and the homey smell of just-popped corn, and there was not a single beer can in the recycling bin.

"I love it here," Mary told me in a hushed tone so the tour guide could not hear that they were about to hook another student.

Then I saw a twenty-year-old guy just exiting the shower walking directly through our group, wearing only a towel. "Coming through, excuse me." He was parting our tour group in two, like Moses in terry cloth.

A genuine glimpse of college life. I was intrigued that the surfer dude was so comfortable that he could parade barefoot and practically naked past forty total strangers. Then it hit me—it was three thirty on a Thursday afternoon at a Catholic college, in a *girls'* dorm.

Boy in towel + girls' dorm = over my dead body.

Why didn't the admissions office warn students, "We've got prospective applicants coming through this afternoon; please wear pants"?

During their high school junior years, my children started asking us to take them on college tours across the country. We would spend hours listening to dynamic student salesmen as they described meal plans, campus parking, and Wi-Fi hot spots, all while walking backward.

In the almost thirty years since I'd gone to college a lot changed. On my first freshman day at the University of Kansas, I registered for classes, opened my first bank account, and met a blond girl at a dance in the dorm parking lot who showed me how cute she could be by puking her guts out in my lobby's garbage can.

"You okay?" It sounded like I was worried. In reality, I just hoped she would not notice that I was not using either her first or her last name, both of which I'd forgotten thirty seconds after we met. It had been a mistake for my roommate to invite her over to our dorm, and I could tell by how fast she was drinking that sloe gin, and by how much, that she was clearly a party girl who probably grew up playing with Divorce Barbie, which came with all of Ken's stuff.

"It's probably just the liquor talking," I said, but she snoozed through whatever I had to say. That very morning my own father had told me to make the most of my college days because I was the first member of my entire family tree ever to enroll in college, and he wanted me to experience something that he never got the chance to.

"Need a Tic Tac?" had been a thoughtful question on my part, but that night I learned that the alcoholically comatose generally don't worry about how minty fresh their breath is.

Suddenly I felt more than a little guilty that my parents had trusted me to be responsible, and there I was with a newfound independence I'd never imagined, as evidenced by the deeply breathing blonde who just needed a chalk outline. It was one of those "You're not in Kansas anymore" moments, but I was still in Kansas.

"Dorothy . . . ?" Was her name Dorothy? Debbie? Denise? Darn it, never mind.

Why did I go to the University of Kansas? Easy. I was almost a native, and with my grades they had to let me in. I entertained the idea of an exclusive school in the East, but my parents insisted that they

could never afford to send me anywhere past St. Louis, so I passed
on the chance to go Ivy, where I would certainly have inexplicably
affected a Belgian accent.

Instead I went to KU, where, thanks to my family's income level, I
got grants and scholarships and loans, and I was able to work my way
through college, eventually graduating with distinction, magna cum
lucky. My Western Civilization instructor told me at the conclusion
of his class, "You, sir, have the greatest vocabulary I've ever heard." I
thanked him for the compliment but made a mental note that he was
from Pakistan.

When I became a father myself, I discovered that nothing pro-
claimed that you were a successful parent more than the window
sticker of a really prestigious college in the back of the station wagon.
Harvard, Princeton, and Yale all trump Hooterville State University,
which would not impress anybody unless your neighbor is Larry the
Cable Guy.

Still in his high school junior year, our son, Peter, seemed content
to live at home forever with no interest in leaving the cocoon. Eventually we forced him to sit down and draw up a list of schools. He really
didn't care about his future academic career. At that point he would
have put down College of Cardinals and filed for early admission.

"Hey, it says here you have to be a priest!" he'd realize, filling out
the College of Cardinals application. "I don't want to be a priest.
They work weekends."

Eventually a list was drawn up, a series of campus tours was made,
as his mother wore off five thousand miles of tire tread so that he
could eventually winnow his favorites down to two.

"Let the brownnosing begin."

At one of the top schools in America I was told point-blank, "Relax, he's in." That from a university official who had that week do-
nated a million dollars to the school. Not leaving anything to chance,
I also ingratiated myself with one of that university's most powerful
graduates, who at that moment was mounting a run for president of
the United States. His letter of recommendation arrived on impres-

sive U.S. Senate stationery; we knew that it was the icing on the college cake. April first, at five in the afternoon, I logged on to their .edu website and got the good news.

"Admission denied. Have a good day."

This same school had all but promised another family that their student son would also be admitted, and with that they wrote a one-million-dollar donation for an open-ended research program where students probably stand in lab coats and watch *Oprah*. That rich kid also was denied, *after the check was cashed.* Cue up the theme song to *Shaft.*

Luckily Peter's other first choice, Villanova, said yes, and invited him to spend the next four years in the leafy suburbs of Philadelphia. As a parent I was filled with a stratospheric sense of pride as I applied the prestigious Villanova sticker above the defogger strips in the back window of our car. Of course we would no longer be able to buy gasoline, because that sticker would cost me $42,703 a year for the next four years, not including stuffed-crust pizza.

Years earlier I lost track of the number of times I'd wake up in the middle of the night, doing college tuition computations: "Three kids, four years each . . ." Then I'd move a decimal point in my head, content to know that my deserving children would all get world-class educations, and all I'd have to do is sell one kidney.

"I forgot to tell you when you got home," my wife said middinner. "I mailed his tuition yesterday." That sent a jolt of electricity directly to my gizzard. It wasn't due for two months.

"You did what?"

I'd been doing mental gymnastics figuring how I'd eventually finance college by borrowing money from my 401(k) and then transferring it into my checking account at the last possible moment, but my wife short-circuited the entire process with a check she wrote on the way to pick up the dry cleaning.

"I paid early because I didn't want them to change their minds," she said, and it seemed to make perfect sense, so I excused myself to do some emergency online banking.

"I thought we were going to check with the bursar's office to see if we could pay with bonus miles."

The money part was terrifying only until it was time actually to start college, when a lifetime of a parent's hopes and dreams and fears amount to a single haphazard pyramid of clean laundry, desk lamps, and cheesy crackers piled on the curb in front of a dorm. Just as Kathy dropped him off for his first day of kindergarten, my wife was the one who dropped him off at college as he made the official transition from our house to frat house. Kathy called me every half hour with updates, but the most wrenching was her final report: After a prayer for the students everybody said good-bye to their students only to get into their cars and pull out at exactly the same time. Stuck in a colossal traffic jam, there was not one horn honking.

"Everybody in every car is crying," she whispered.

"He'll be back. He needs stuff," I assured her, which was easy for me because I was six thousand miles away with his sisters, still on vacation. Her heart was broken, so I reminded her, "It's only three weeks until you see him again. We'll be there for parents' weekend."

It was there that I was introduced to Peter's roommates, which was in itself surprising because he was supposed to have only one. They were very nice guys, but the dorm room was built for two humans. Due to an enrollment boom, three testosterone factories would be holed up in a nonventilated twelve-by-fifteen cinder-block room for an entire academic year. In college terms it's referred to as a forced triple; it should really be called a sinus volcano.

Disillusioned at Peter's being warehoused in a small room for a year with two guys, I tried some positive spin. "It's college, not a Canyon Ranch spa," I said. Then I did the math in my head, and four years at Canyon Ranch would actually cost me less than this place.

When I stood up from his desk chair at the end of my first dorm visit I discovered that I'd unwittingly sat on a damp towel and the crotch of my khaki pants was soaked, which explained why for his first two semesters Peter's friends would refer to me as "the Depends dad."

Thus started Peter's career in college. He got great grades in every class except Italian, for the simple reason that those confounding people in Italy insist on not speaking English.

A towering six five now, he is regarded as literally the big man on campus: an announcer at the basketball games, active in the fraternity scene, student politics, and the college radio station. So we were surprised when he reported that he was outright barred from entering an important lecture.

"Why can't I go in?"

"Sold out," the guy with the walkie-talkie told Peter.

Whom would college kids stand in line to see and hear? An aging radical or dissident? A skinny despot from a dangerous country building a nuke reactor? No and no, Peter was not allowed to see the band Hanson.

"Full house. One more and the fire marshal will close us down," the security guard told him, waving him away, but Peter would not take no for an answer.

Hanson's song "MMMBop" had been the single tune at our house that all three of our kids of various ages could sing together, because that was all there was to the lyric: "Mmm bop, Mmm bop." With his childhood idols just on the other side of that closed door, he knew something he could do to crash the gate. He dashed up the hill to the campus bookstore, where he bought the fattest, blackest marker manufactured. Then in what I would like to think was the first time he'd ever stripped to the waist in the dining hall restroom, he practiced tracing some words across his chest. Confident that he had the spacing right, he took the cap off the marker, stared into the mirror, and wrote nipple to nipple *Hanson #1*. It was big and bold, and why wouldn't it be? He'd used the Sanford Magnum 44 Permanent Marker. The 44 apparently stood for the IQ of a college kid who would write the name of an aging boy band on his chest.

"You don't see that every day," one of two dozen visiting priests said as my shirtless son speed-walked across the quad past their tour group. Surely they were thinking that he was a wayward young sinner who'd made many bad choices in life and that was why on this, the coldest day of the year, he was walking around with some devil-message chest tattoo. If he'd been strung out on heroin or a speed-ball, the priests would have stopped to straighten him out, but the free buffet lunch in the president's conference room was about to start, and they didn't want to miss the appetizers.

"Now can I come in?" he asked the arena guard who'd shooed him away fifteen minutes earlier. The guard forsook his fire marshal threat, and surprisingly, Peter was admitted through a stage door, and found himself instantly the focal point of six thousand female Hanson fans.

"Hey, come here," a total stranger beckoned, turning his camera phone Peter's direction. "I want a picture with the *Almost Naked Hanson Fan.*"

As soon as they posed, a wave of applause swept across the giant room. Sensing that his audacious stunt was being warmly received, Peter shut his eyes and blew a kiss toward all, Sinatra style, and then took a deep and dramatic bow, and with that the applause crescen-doed into a deafening tribute. Too bad it wasn't for him.

The Hanson brothers had entered through another stage door, and every set of eyes in the place was on them, not my son, who was basking in the applause. Returning upright, Peter saw that everybody in the facility was facing the other end of the stage, and he became as embarrassed as a person who was stripped to the waist could pos-sibly be.

Taking a chair, he was delighted to be inside with the pop idols of his childhood. After an hour his bliss turned to boredom. Hanson did not sing. They did not dance. His Magic Marker self-mutilation had gotten him a ringside seat for a mind-numbingly lifeless presentation about the accounting problems of independent record producing.

MMmmm boring!

Permanent black Magic Marker ink does not come off with a squirt of Neutrogena; two or three showers a day for a week and it was still visible on his rib cage. For a kid who'd grown up listening to Hanson,

TALES FROM THE Dad SIDE

he'd moved on musically and was in fact a rap music aficionado, taking part in a weekly "rap-off" where he would compete against the other lyrical impresarios, many of whom were on the school's nationally ranked basketball team. Imagine ten of the tallest young men on campus standing in the hall of a dorm, with a boom box rhythm track blaring as they all tried to outdo one another's rhyming and rapping, and for some enigmatic reason all of the guys were shirtless. Apparently rapping was easier if the artist was not encumbered with a shirt that could ride up on his creativity.

"Hey, Slim," a future NBA multimillionaire asked, "what's up with your chest?" pointing to my son's torso, which still had the remnants of the Hanson ink. Peter thought the Lava soap had taken off the ink, and most of his skin, but to his chagrin it was still visible to the naked eye.

"This?" he asked, pointing at what was left of the *n* in *Hanson*. "It's a *gang* thing."

My son is six five, with blond hair and blue eyes, a guy whose belts have either lobsters or ponies on them; what *gang* could he possibly have belonged to, the Apple Dumpling Gang?

"How's your son loving college?" a university official asked me during his visit to my New York office. Usually that would be a proud parent's chance to crow about his child's achievements; I on the other hand felt like I was filling out a survey for J. D. Power and Associates and knew it was important to be truthful.

"To be honest, he's in a forced triple, a room that is dark and damp, next door to the laundry room, so every fifteen minutes when somebody's white load is done it buzzes and wakes him up all night long. The room is also directly across the hall from the men's restroom, a facility so ghastly that legend has it somebody from the class of '03 died from some flesh-eating bacteria while flossing."

That was not the answer he was expecting. "But other than that, I bet he's having a great year?" He should have stopped while he was ahead.

"Actually, one of his roommates is up all night under his blanket

talking to his girlfriend at another university on a webcam. So between the laundry buzzer, that odious men's room, and the lonely
guy making a booty call, my son has not had one good night's sleep
so far this year." The college executive grimaced as if I'd just skied
naked into a tea party with the pope.

"Your son's story is proof we need to build more dorms." He was
right, and I nodded my approval. "That's why we're in the midst of our
three-hundred-million-dollar-endowment drive." He then pulled out
an impressive presentation with my name personally engraved upon
it and made a pitch to me as if I were buying a time-share. "Let
me show you the difference you can make by joining the President's
Club," he continued, trying a new way of asking for thousands of
dollars. Was he kidding? Was there a hidden camera somewhere? Apparently my son's "dorm of the damned" story was a useful segue into
the importance of contributing more. At that moment I was spending on college almost fifty thousand dollars that year, and would be
shelling out fifty grand more the next and the next and the next.
Each year I was essentially buying a Lexus that I would never drive.

"I'd love to help, but I'm in cable."

"Yes, we watch you every morning," he said, figuring that since his
cable bill was $125 a month, I was personally getting most of that.

Now that Peter is in his final year of college, I am amazed at how
much he has grown. He's off campus in an apartment that his roommates have decorated with a poster of John Belushi from *Animal
House* flipping the bird, opposite a poster of Will Ferrell lovingly
holding a blow-up doll. One of his roommates is twenty-one, so it
was certainly that kid's half-gallon bottle of vodka in the freezer, and
the recycling bin was overflowing with his dead Coors cans.

"Did you see all those beer cans?" my wife asked in a panicked but
hushed voice as we left at the end of parents' weekend.

"I did," I said, completely calm, amazed at how much I'd changed
in four short years. "Isn't it great—they're recycling!"

Mary, our second child, is now in college, and her first-day drop-
off was just like our son's; after everything was unloaded from the

car, there were long hugs, and plenty of tears, and then the parents pulled out simultaneously for a titanic traffic jam where nobody was in a hurry to leave the children they'd raised. Every mom and dad and sibling looking straight ahead, crying. Kathy and I know for a fact that the hardest thing in the English language that a parent will ever say to a child is "good-bye."

Now that we've installed a second child in college, I've had a chance to think back nostalgically to the seventies, when there were fewer diseases and lower drinking ages, and pants were supposed to be worn that tight. I remember leaving home that first day: I gave my mother and father each a squeeze before I climbed into my dangerously overloaded Ford Pinto and, with sufficient promises to call the instant I arrived, put the car in drive and started up the on-ramp of life.

I had put on the brave face, but I could feel real tears hanging off my nose. Pulling out, I stared at my parents in the rearview mirror; public displays of affection were rare, but there was my father with his arm around my mom's shoulders supporting her as she hugged him. I'd never seen them like that before, and never saw them do that again. Maybe that was how they used to embrace twenty years before, when they were first in love, and I was just a twinkle.

I'd looked forward to that day of independence for a long time, and suddenly my good-byes were over, and I was on my way, and I felt like I had a hole in my heart. The oldest child, the one my father called five times a day to help him do whatever he needed, was suddenly gone.

"That's what you're supposed to do," my father told me before I left. "Kids grow up and they leave." And once again he was right, because I never moved back.

I hope that when they're through with college, all of my kids move back, either to live in our house or at least to live nearby. We invested so much time, patience, and chicken fingers in them; it would be nice to admire our handiwork without making an airplane trip somewhere.

To sweeten the pot, I've told them they wouldn't have to pay us rent, ever. Of course, if they wanted to take us out to dinner and then maybe to a show like one by the legendary performer Wayne Newton, we wouldn't say no. All we'd need is twenty minutes' notice, so I could shower, shave, and strip to the waist and scrawl in Magic Marker *Wayne* nipple to nipple, which I can do faster than you can say "Danke schoen."

21

Pride

Dad, Stop Pushing Me Around!

I t was a busy morning. My father and I had already been to Home Depot and the tile place, and now we'd pulled in for the last stop on our errand list, the grocery store. He had strained something in his lower back, so he got out of the car very carefully. Walking, he was so wooden that he made Al Gore look like Freddie Mercury.

"We won't need that cart, Dad," I said as he slowly and carefully pulled a shopping trolley out of the cart corral.

Suddenly he froze in place. I figured he'd pulled too hard and hurt his back. That was not the case. Like Indiana Jones finally eyeballing the lost ark, my father was staring at this line of a hundred shopping carts because on the front of each and every one of them was a full color photograph of his son holding high a piece of cinnamon swirl raisin toast while promoting the *Fox & Friends* program on the Fox News Channel.

"Holy cow, that's you!" he blurted out in the same jaw-dropping voice a person would use if he'd walked in on the family wirehaired terrier applying over the phone for a Visa card.

The cart promotion ran three months and had ended the month before, but this store apparently hadn't got the new Tropicana posters to paste over my face, so that was why I'd completely forgotten about it.

"That's a very good picture!" His voice was dripping with pride. I'd heard him sound like that only a handful of times: at my wedding, upon the birth of my children, and in high school when I pulled off a wrestling upset and pinned the scariest 118-pound man to ever wear a unitard.

"That's my son," he announced in full show-off mode to the produce guy, who did not instantly make the connection that I was on the cart. So my father pointed at the cart, and back at me, just for the benefit of Mr. Arugula.

"Dad, don't," I begged, knowing he would badger the man in the apron until the employee realized who I was and ran through the aisles of the store screaming, "The face on that shopping cart is *ALIVE!*"

As a father, I understood the pride of my father, which he tried to explain away as something else. "Stephen, I'm just trying to get you a little publicity."

Okay, that was one way to spin it, or maybe he was fishing for somebody to say, "Oh, that young man on the cart is your son? Then you must be a really good father, to have raised a man who has nice skin and is not addicted to offtrack betting. I'll call the Nobel Peace Prize people about nominating you as Father of the Year." Next thing you knew, my father would be in Oslo chatting up Jimmy Carter types and eating pickled fish parts.

Whatever his motivation, I made sure we speed-walked through the store. But my father still did his nonverbal best to get other shoppers to notice me. He pushed the cart directly at a person by the dairy case and at another in the breakfast food aisle kamikaze style so they'd get a head-on view of my picture, and then he veered away at the last possible second. Then he took a comical double take at my picture and then directly at me. Nobody said anything—they probably just saw a distinguished man in a Burberry trench coat staring bug-eyed at a blond guy walking briskly ahead of him.

Probably some sort of a drug interaction, passersby would think, wondering if the younger man was a male nurse, just taking the older gent to the store for a field trip. "Must be from the bin if he's so happy to see a cart."

With the three items I'd sought now on the checkout belt, I was ready to make this as quick as possible. Sensing I'd pushed his mute button, my father stood quietly as I wrote a check for the exact amount and scribbled our home phone on the memo line.

"Check-cashing card," the gum-chewing cashier announced.

Shoving my hand in my pocket to pull out my keys, I instantly saw I had a problem on my hands—I'd inadvertently picked up my wife's key ring, which did not have our check card on it. "I don't have it. Can't you use my phone number?"

"Go over to the customer-service booth. They'll look up your number." The clerk then picked up a *National Enquirer* to read about the latest starlet who was playing hide the moussaka with some Greek shipping heir. "I'll wait," he said.

Blood pressure rising, I felt thoroughly insulted. I'd been to that store once a week for the last ten years. As my annoyance morphed into rage, I blurted out something I've heard many other people say but I've never had the reason or the inclination to announce: "I think you know who I am. . . ."

The clerk looked up, scanned my face, shook his head no, and returned to the *Enquirer*. Getting more steamed, I knew that if he ever planted that nose of his in *TV Guide* instead of that tabloid crap, he'd know I was on global television at least two hours a day, the host of the number one cable morning news show, the guy Jon Stewart and Stephen Colbert skewered on a nightly basis. I was no fringe character known as Lonelyguy49 on the Internet with only seven Facebook friends; I was on the number one cable morning news show on the planet. Gosh darn it, I'm the host with the toast!

"I come here all the time. You've probably seen me on television," I said in a cheery voice, trying to be pleasant although I really wanted to clunk him upside the head with my two-pound London broil.

"I don't have a TV," he said. "Do you want me to call a manager?"

And then, like so many times before, my father intervened to help his struggling son. "Give him a break. He works here."

"No he doesn't," snapped back the cashier. "He's on TV."

"I thought you didn't watch," I interjected.

"Well, if he doesn't work here," my father observed, "then why's he on *your company cart*?" It was a Perry Mason gotcha moment as the guy in the paper hat examined the ad and then turned toward me.

"How'd you do that?"

"Doesn't matter. You're going to take his check and we're going to leave," my father instructed like a hypnotist would say, "and when I snap my fingers you'll have no memory of what just took place." And that's exactly what happened. The cashier took the check and we left.

I felt a little bad that I'd given my dad a hard time about my picture on the cart; he was simply doing what all parents love to do, brag on their kids. Their pride is a triumphant validation that they did something right while raising us. There are few times in life as satisfying as when you realize that a parent is proud of you. It feels great when you're twelve years old, and even better when you're fifty.

"Dad, none of that would have happened if you would have paid the twenty-three bucks for me," I said halfway through the parking lot, and then I abruptly realized I was alone. My father was standing back at the cart corral using a ballpoint pen to pry my picture out of the black plastic frame.

"I'm taking this home," he said, rolling it up treasure-map style.

If the cart police took inventory that night, three pictures were MIA. Incidentally, I don't take my father to that store anymore; while there is no statute of limitations on pride, there is one on vandalism, and until it runs out in eighteen months, we'll have to double-coupon elsewhere.

22

Emotion

Daddy's Mascara Is Running

My daughter Sally has already made it clear that when she is a billionaire, she will sequester her mother and me in a three-bedroom villa somewhere on the fifty-acre, five-star resort she's going to own and operate with Barron Trump, the Donald's son, who is currently under five years old. I believe Sally really means it, so I have taken her pledge as an opportunity to spend whatever money I have saved for retirement on Sudoku books.

The desire to somehow repay your parents is universal; it's an urge that goes back to when Noah was in third grade. "Someday I'm going to get you a *big boat*," he promised his beaming parents. Unbeknownst to them, they'd one day share it with barnyard animals.

When I was Sally's age, I dreamed of saying thanks to my parents with a new car or a big house, but my first full-time job paid four dollars and ten cents an hour, and on that salary all I could afford was a board game, which meant I'd have to think less yacht and more Yahtzee!

My father was the one I wanted to take care of first. The hardest-working man I'd ever seen, he sometimes worked two or three jobs to support us. Never spending much on himself, he made do with whatever he had. He was a handy man who never once called a plumber or an electrician or a carpenter when something at our house needed fixing, because he'd figure out how to do it himself. His only lament: "I could do this better and faster if I had the right tools."

My first payday was on a Thursday. The next day I walked into the Topeka Sears store, where America shops for its parents, and found exactly what my father had dreamed of for years: a three-horsepower, ten-inch radial arm saw. A mechanical cutting marvel, it also came with an automatic brake that would stop it in a flash, which was good because it was treacherous. I learned how much so from my wood-shop teacher when I asked him how many dowels to put in the side of a project, and he shouted "Five" over the buzz of a table saw and for emphasis flashed his open hand my way with every finger and thumb standing up, all three of them.

I drove the ninety miles to my parents' house and unloaded my surprise with no fanfare. I'd quietly clued in my blabbermouth sisters, and my payback was set.

"Dad, come here!" I hollered toward the garage, and when he arrived in the living room our entire family had gathered in a semicircle around something bulky under a blanket. "I gotcha something."

I'd seen that semigoofy grin of his many times in the past when we'd make similar presentations. We didn't have much disposable income, and he insisted we not spend any money on him, so we'd wrap up and give him something that he already owned. That's right, we invented regifting.

Another recycled something was surely what he thought it was until he tugged off the blanket to reveal the most expensive Crafts-man radial arm saw I could afford. It would take me three years to pay it off, but it was worth every single minimum payment due.

"Oh, Stephen . . . ," was all he said before his eyes got glassy, then wet, and as he pulled the saw across the deck toward him, a single tear rolled right off his face onto a sticker warning to pick up severed fingers when you were done woodworking. That was a milestone; it was only the second time I'd ever seen him cry. "Thanks," was all he could choke out.

Scanning the room, I saw that my mother and four sisters all had tears in their eyes too.

Twenty years earlier, we were driving through Grand Island, Nebraska, on the hottest day of the year, and the engine fan chose that day and time to unbolt itself from the motor and spin directly into the radiator, resulting in a yellow-green gusher of steam and anti-freeze that literally hit the fan.

"You're looking at three hundred," Mr. Goodwrench flat out told my father, who'd struggled to come up with the money to cover breakfast that morning at a greasy spoon near Omaha.

"Well, I have to get these kids home, so you better fix it," my dad said with a sigh, and the guy in the coveralls turned to repair our radiator. My father walked outside the radiator shop and stood under a big oak, probably to figure out how he'd pay for this, because he didn't have that kind of money. That was at a time when people didn't have any credit cards; he had only a wad of cash that after a week visiting his family was down to mostly fives and a few tens.

My mom fished a couple of nickels out of her purse and told my sisters to buy some sodas. They were giddy at the prospect of spending hours in an unfamiliar place with thirty thousand dirty things to stick in their mouths. They repeatedly asked my mom to use the filthiest washroom I'd ever seen, which in my second-grade imagination was littered with the carcasses of the health department inspectors who'd keeled over when exposed to a biologically infectious urinal cake.

My dad looked so lonely under that tree, I walked out to see if he wanted a sip of my Dr Pepper. I said something about how hot it was as I walked up behind him, but he didn't turn toward me, which was weird. So I took another step and stood in front of him, where I noticed to my horror that he had a couple of big tears hanging on his chin. When he turned toward me, I snapped my head away, ashamed that I'd barged into his private moment. He put a hand on my shoulder and said, "Don't worry. It's going to be okay." I wasn't worried, because my dad always took care of everything, but now seeing that the strongest man in the world could cry like everybody else, I didn't feel so good.

"Let me have a sip of that," was the last thing I heard before he drank my Dr Pepper dry. The car was fixed later that day, and we drove home. Forty years later my father told me what happened that day; he explained to the mechanic that he didn't have the money, but he promised he'd send him a check when he got home, which he did because a promise was a promise.

December 25, 1997, I was with my wife and kids at our home in New Jersey when the phone rang at 4 A.M. It was my sister. My mom had died. On Christmas. I jumped out of bed and packed a bag, and Kathy booked me a flight. Because Christmas was always supposed to be the happiest day on the calendar, the one day our kids looked forward to all year, my wife and I sat in the dark waiting to wake them up, and then videotaped them running down the stairs to see what Santa had left. I was on the airplane flying back to Kansas before Kathy explained what had happened. Never in their lives had my children known a person who had died. When my wife and kids flew out for the funeral, my littlest one's, Sally's, only funeral experience was from watching Princess Diana's on television.

"Why isn't anybody throwing flowers?" Sally asked as the hearse solemnly pulled away from the church. They threw flowers for Diana, why not Grandma?

My mom's funeral was the first time my children ever saw me cry. As I started writing this story, I remembered the times I'd seen my father cry, and thought about how composed I'd always been around my own children, trying to maintain a sphinxish manner when dealing with sad matters. Driving to the grocery store with Sally who was now a high school freshman, I asked her how she'd feel if she ever saw me crying again.

"Whaddaya mean *if*?" she said.

"Really? When?" I was suddenly defensive, knowing nobody had ever given me a radial arm saw.

"At the movies."

She'd hit paydirt. Sitting in the dark, it was easy to get caught up in a story. Those Hollywood screenwriters knew exactly how to push my buttons. So I asked *what* movies, expecting her to say *Schindler's List* or *Steel Magnolias*.

"The *first time*?" She paused for a moment, and I could see she was rewinding something in her head, probably remembering how I was overcome by the raw emotion of *Dying Young* or *Titanic*.

Her answer was accurate and devastating. "It was *A Bug's Life*."

In my own defense, *A Bug's Life* is a heartbreaking movie when the little ant needs help to keep his ant farm from being wiped out. Then Sally added a coda. "Actually, Daddy, you cry at *all* the movies."

"Like . . . ?"

"Like *Finding Nemo, The Little Mermaid, Beauty and the Beast*." I was surprised she had a Roger Ebert–like list at the ready of her dad's favorite tearjerkers. Who wouldn't cry at those Disney classics that feature an orange striped fish trying to find his dad, a mermaid who combs her hair with a fork, and a beautiful ingenue who talks to candelabras?

It was now official—I was a softy. Later that night at dinner, I asked my entire family if, aside from at the movies, they had ever seen me cry, because nobody had ever said a word.

"Every Sunday," Mary, the high school senior, announced, which made me wonder, Sunday? The only thing we did every Sunday was church, and while there were a couple of hymns that got me every time, we didn't sing "Amazing Grace" every week.

Seeing I was struggling, Mary solved the mystery: "Sunday nights, *Extreme Makeover: Home Edition*."

Until that moment, I had thought any sentimentality I'd done was in private. But apparently if there's even a whiff of something emotional, my entire family sneaks a glance my way to see if the show has officially risen to the red-eye level, like a Hallmark ad.

Real men do cry. In the movie *Ocean's Thirteen*, two of the con men, played by George Clooney and Brad Pitt, get weepy as they watch an episode of *Oprah* when she builds a house for a family who has nothing, exactly like my favorite show. Finally, I had something in common with Clooney and Pitt, aside from us all being international sex symbols.

I've evolved to the point where I think it's okay to show humility and humanity. Feelings are the only things that separate us from the animals. Surprisingly, my own kids are not weepers. I could go through a half box of Kleenex watching an *Old Yeller* marathon, and my children's only reaction would be, "That dog didn't really die, did it? It's just a movie, right?" Once assured that the dog, a member of the Screen Actors Guild, was just playing dead, they'd adjourn to the kitchen to toast the dog's continued good health with snacks. I could remind them that the movie was made fifty years ago and the dog has been dead since the 1960s, but I would never rain on their parade.

Meanwhile, my wife, Kathy, is much more evolved than I. When I asked Sally what made Mommy cry, it took her most of a day to remember the first time she saw my wife shed a tear.

"*The Country Bears* movie."

Thank goodness, somebody stable was on hand to wear the pantsuit at our house.

23

Landmarks

The Innings and Outings of Life

Some boys become men when they join the marines or on their honeymoon night. Always trying to take the road less traveled, I became a man at a Chinese restaurant.

Kansas is a state where salad bars uniquely feature chocolate cake and a simmering kettle of gravy, so anything off our regular caveman red meat diet was always appreciated, and that's why Mars Chinese on the west side of Salina was one of my family's favorite places. The Mars family knew Kansans were hopelessly addicted to starches, and that's why they always had one additional table item that I've never seen in any Chinatown: a quarter loaf of Wonder bread.

"I'll pick that up when you're ready," the waitress with chopsticks in her hair said, dropping off the bill.

And with that my father launched into an oft-told story about a guy he met on an army troopship who was assigned to kitchen duty and, during rough seas, threw up into the scrambled eggs. As my sisters grimaced, I realized something was wrong—my father, who was always in a hurry to leave, hadn't budged. Usually when the waitress brought the bill he'd say, "Here you go," and pay her in cash on the spot before she had time to walk away.

"So this guy took the egg beater, mixed 'em up, and then cooked it!" At which point his tale got a gagging look from my sister Lisa.

Why wasn't my dad picking up the bill? Let's go and get out of here. He knew it was there—I'd seen him eyeball it when the wait-

ress dropped it off. Yet he just sat there yakking away. Did he want
another cookie; was this one of the early stages of dementia? Then I
got an awful feeling in the pit of my stomach as it dawned on me: *he
wanted me to pay.*

That meal was at my suggestion to celebrate my new job in Wich-
ita, where I was pulling in a substantial eighteen grand a year, which
my father thought was a lot for a single kid with no student loans.
Why not? I thought as I slid the brown fake leather folder that was
parked in front of my father over to my side and opened it to assess
the financial damage.

"What are you doing, Stephen?" my mom asked.

"I'm paying."

"No you're not. Jim, pick that up."

"If he wants to," my dad said, as if it were a teachable moment.
"He's got a job. He can handle it."

Initially I was a little offended that my father wanted me to take
care of the bill, but as he argued with my mom, I oddly *wanted* to pick
it up. It was a sign that I wasn't just a kid anymore; I was an official
taxpaying, paycheck-cashing breadwinner, and that day the bread
was Wonder.

The bill was twenty-nine dollars. I used a credit card, and five
ones for the tip. My father was beaming: *My son can afford to throw
around five dollars.* My mother, however, was less altruistic. "That's
too much," and she took two bills off the pile and stuffed them into
my shirt pocket as we left the restaurant the day I became a man.

That was when life was simple, but then things sped up. I got married, had kids, big jobs, and bigger problems. Where did the time
go? It seemed like just yesterday I was a wild and crazy college kid
who'd get up for breakfast during *60 Minutes.* I blinked, and now I
was wearing the daddy pants, as a father of three, with a wife who'd
occasionally remind me of her love by telling me it was time to trim
my nose hairs, "Unless you want me to braid them."

While I may feel like an antique, my children keep me young and
on my toes, especially with my reputation as the Mr. Answer Man of

the family. Rather than actually find answers in their textbooks, they just bark out questions, and I bounce back accurate answers.

"Hey, Dad, the country of Siam is now known as . . . what?"

Once, I was able to confidently spit out the answers with the speed and precision of Alex Trebek hopped up on an Italian espresso speedball, but as my kids entered middle school, things were getting mixed up in my head.

"Daddy, Siam . . ."

My reputation as the family's walking, talking human encyclopedia teetering, I remembered that Siam is the setting for *The King and I* and that Siam is the root of "Siamese," but that's not a country, it's a cat. I closed my eyes and took an educated guess based upon the fact that they sound alike. "Siam is now Ceylon," I confidently hedged.

"Very funny, Daddy! It's Thailand."

Geographic trivia was hard because the world kept changing. I was still an expert at the basics until my son, Peter, asked me for help with high school physics, and as he verbally announced his equation, all I could see was numbers with arrows at the end pointing to other numbers. Stupefied, I did the only thing a father could do: I hired a physics tutor.

As my children's homework got harder, the trips to Dad slowed to a trickle, and instead the kids asked one another. What happened? I wondered, thinking back to the time when I could rattle off all fifty state capitals, and even name the U.S. president who invented the folding chair.

The mental acuity was bound to fade, but I would always be the biggest and the strongest member of the family because my girls weren't WNBA material and their brother was only five eight his junior year. At his age I was already six one, so he was destined to always stand in the shadow of his father, where he belonged. Inexplicably, the next year my boy grew an astonishing eight inches. It was at that time that I seriously questioned whether the makers of chicken fingers had replaced Crisco with human growth hormone.

To camouflage the fact that I was no longer the tallest, I refused to be photographed next to him unless seated, and at church, our only weekly joint appearance, I would motion for him to walk to the altar first, followed by his vastly shorter sisters and mother, before I'd bring up the rear. The girls created a visual buffer during that walk for Communion, which heightwise was like a police lineup, with genuflecting.

His son is half a head taller. Next thing you know, Steve'll be bald, the monsignor surely thought every time he placed bread in the hands of the height-challenged dad.

While my own father was baldish, the substantial hair loss thing would never happen—and if it did I'd get plugs, a hair-replacement system, or as a last resort one of those Eva Gabor wigs that my mother's friend Nancy wore, and which she said were easier to shampoo than real hair because she washed them in the dishwasher. Just to be safe, later tonight I'll look on the KitchenAid site for the correct setting for wavy blond.

A tough year for the family alpha male. I could no longer help my son with his homework, he was half a head taller, and all I had left on my side was sheer strength. I could still beat him in a footrace from the street to the garage, and when we'd lift our big ladder to clean out the gutters, he could not keep it steady; I was clearly the Schwarzenegger member of the family. To remind him of that known fact, I challenged him to a duel.

We were watching March Madness; my alma mater, Kansas, had just gotten whupped by my son's Villanova team. I protested and said that the game was a fluke. Then, stacking the deck in my favor, I told him that the best way to determine the better team was for us to wrestle. I'd been a respectable high school wrestler, and I scored two points on a tricky takedown, his spindly frame making a dull thud on the hardwood floor as his mother commanded, "Peter, don't hurt your father."

She was a real laugh riot, because I was in the process of proving that I was still the family's top dog. At eighteen years old he could drive a car, go to college, kiss girls when necessary, but he could not possibly overpower his father, who, at age fifty, was 175 pounds of twisted steel and sex appeal.

I smiled as I dominated him and asked him if he'd had enough. "No," he spat, and he continued to thrash beneath me until one of his much longer arms hooked me and I was suddenly wedged between the couch and our Pottery Barn console table, which looked better in the catalog without a middle-aged man's head pitifully crushed up against its rich mahogany veneer. I had one other immediate observation as I lay there: *I CAN'T BREATHE!*

A weird sleeper hold was now in danger of cutting off the air supply to my brain. Wiggling around and throwing my legs every which way except toward our brand-new fifty-inch plasma screen, I was in trouble. Resorting to the only thing a man desperate to hold on to his youth would do, I inched into position to give him an illegal kidney punch that would immediately make him let me go. One little wallop and I'd be back on my feet, like Ali standing over Sonny Liston. Then the father voice kicked in. *You can't hurt your own son, you dope,* which was true, because someday I would need him to pay our monthly room and board at a fancy assisted-living home where every Tuesday a former Dallas Cowboys Cheerleader would teach water aerobics.

"You win," I wheezed out in defeat. He peeled himself off me and then gave me a little look, worried he'd broken an important father part. It was a landmark moment as the title of strongest guy in the house was ripped out of the grip of the old man and now belonged to the boy. To his credit, Peter did not rub it in; he simply returned to the television to watch other very tall young men run up and down the court as I wondered how many of them could beat up their fathers. Life had just slapped me in the face with the subtlety of a sock filled with horse manure.

My daughter Mary, an all-around fabulous girl, followed in her brother's scholarly footsteps. A student leader and serious student (the New Jersey Academic Decathlon gold medal winner in Civil War art and silver medalist in economics), she was half a light-year ahead of anything I could help her with homeworkwise. That meant

I was down to one family member whom I could still beat. Sally. She was eleven.

By far the most innocent, every night at bedtime she'd write a note that I'd wake up and read in the morning. It was festooned with stick figures depicting the two of us. I was worried about her many serious misspellings of common words, but relieved knowing she would always be my little jejune ingenue. And then out of nowhere during a routine dinner conversation, Sally protested a point her brother had made.

"That's not relevant!"

So shocking, and so unexpected—the entire table paused momentarily and then burst into spontaneous appreciative applause. "Sally just used *relevant,*" an astonished Mary proudly announced. "And she used it correctly!"

Uh-oh. Her use of a big word in everyday conversation had to be a fluke. Just like the wild idea that given plenty of time, a thousand monkeys with typewriters would eventually bang out all the works of Shakespeare. In real life, researchers left a computer keyboard in a cage full of monkeys for a month, and all they did was type a lot of *s*'s and *d*'s, two letters not found in Romeo or Juliet. Sally had surely parroted "relevant" as something she had heard on *Hannah Montana.* That was my firmly held belief until one evening I walked into the kitchen as her mother asked her to get a box of noodles out of a drawer.

"What genre pasta, Mom?"

Genre? I didn't use that in a sentence until I was forty. Check, please; everybody had grown up and passed me by, and suddenly the father figure was feeling not so relevant. The torch had been passed from my generation to my children's, so when given the opportunity to perform at a very public spectacle, I knew it was important that our family be represented by our best athlete.

"Peter, how would you like to throw out the first pitch at a Mets game?" I asked my stronger/taller/smarter son.

Fox & Friends cohost Brian Kilmeade and I had been asked to throw out the ceremonial first pitch at Shea, but before we agreed, we huddled and asked if our sons could have the honor. The Mets didn't care, so I asked Peter to do the honor.

"Are you kidding?" my son screamed, accepting the challenge.

Thus started ten days of intensive practice for *the Pitch*. He'd been a solid high school and American Legion ballplayer, but it's a long ways from the chalk circle in the dirt field at Coolidge School to the pitching rubber at Shea Stadium. In my mind I could see him standing there, throwing out the ball to a thunderous ovation and getting a Triple-A contract and a shoe deal before one of the Jersey Boys belted out the national anthem.

We practiced for hours each day after school, and what I realized was that sixty feet is a long way to throw something in front of tens of thousands of strangers with any kind of precision, and suddenly my great idea was haunting me—what if he bounces it, or it flies over the catcher's head? This single toss had the possibility of being the most embarrassing thing he'd ever done in public, and if that happened, whom would he have to thank? His father.

"You don't have to do it," I told him the evening of *the Pitch* as we walked out of the tunnel under the stadium into the bluish white television lights.

Peter said nothing, and I could tell he was freaked out. We stood in the on-deck circle, and as the public address announcer said his name, I shook his hand, and it was wringing wet. Now I worried that the ball would slip out of his sweaty palm. A Zapruder moment. I remember every single frame of what happened next. Having coached baseball, I saw that his ball release was much harder than we'd practiced; obviously it was a case of nerves, meaning it would probably veer wide and paralyze an inattentive batboy, landing my son on the cover of the *New York Post*. Within six months he'd be clinically depressed and addicted to painkillers and living out of the trunk of a car in Queens. I wished I had never asked him to do this. *Peter, why did you have to throw it that hard? That's not the way I would have done it.*

Certainly not—it was a perfect strike.

"Kid, you've got a great cutter," the Mets catcher said as he tossed Peter the game ball.

"Dad, he said *nice cutter!*"

It went unbelievably well, and a cutter at that, whatever that is. Everybody he knew either saw *the Pitch* on television or heard about it, so to commemorate that personal moment, that game ball is encased in a Plexiglas block next to his bed, where our once-a-week cleaning lady promises she'll dust it as soon as hell freezes over.

Exactly one year later I was asked once again to throw out the first pitch, and once again I asked my son, the best athlete in the family.

"Go ahead, Dad, I did it already," was his selflessly mature answer, but then he added, "but you're going to need to practice."

Over the next few days he taught me how to throw a two-seamer, which would be remarkably simple for somebody with full range of shoulder motion, but I was not that person—I've got a hitch in my pitch that makes throwing the ball straight about as unlikely as seeing Rosie O'Donnell on a Thighmaster.

During one practice, my wife came out to the porch to gauge my progress exactly at the moment I threw the ball as hard as I could toward my son's mitt, only to see it hilariously swerve about seventy-five degrees to the left.

"Congratulations," she said. "You're officially YouTube material."

It was hopeless. I knew it, my wife knew it, and unfortunately so did my children, who despite my inability were determined to help me. One week before *My Pitch* I made the sober assessment that no amount of practice would help me throw the ball straight.

"Que sera, sera," I quoted Doris Day, which translated means "I'll move to Mexico if it goes really bad."

My kids continued to beg me to practice over the next few days, but I refused. I was going to wing it. Thirty-eight thousand five hundred people were waiting for my major-league debut. I had just one goal that night, and it was to make sure that I did not bounce the ball; that would horrify my children, who were standing, but not breathing, on the warning track. I walked to the rubber, and paused for the view. This was what John and Paul, George and Ringo, saw when the Beatles played Shea. They were so lucky—all they had to do was sing. At that moment I would have preferred to belt out "Help!" but I wasn't dressed for a musical performance.

Completely calm, because I knew I stank, I raised the ball above my head, wound up a little, took a huge step forward, and let it fly— TWANG went my shoulder. The headline: it did not bounce, crisis averted. Howard Johnson, the famous Met, caught it squarely in his glove, but it was low and outside, which cued the raspberries. If you are one of the seven spectators in attendance who did not boo me, many thanks, and as for the rest of you, I'm a forgiving soul, and you're off the hook for raising the middle finger of contempt in my direction.

As I review my major-league career, the proudest part was that my kids were worried about me, returning the favor of worrying about them for the previous twenty years. There are times when you see your family shift from one stage to the next, but sometimes you find yourself waking up in the seventh-inning stretch, and wonder, Where did the fifth and sixth innings go? Times change, people change. Not so long ago I was carefree and clueless, ultralighting, and booking flights to run with the bulls in Pamplona, but that was long ago and far away, and now I've moved on to my best chapter as a husband and father of three, where my current concept of a wild night on the town is extra breadsticks at the Olive Garden.

"You were great, Daddy!" Sally said after my pitch, grabbing my hand as we walked up the tunnel into my baseball retirement. Maybe I wasn't the strongest or the fastest or the tallest pitcher in our family, but I was the father of the best brownnosers on our block.

"Thanks, Sal," I said. "You just made me feel *relevant* again."

"Feel what?"

A genuine puzzled look on her face—she had clearly forgotten the relevance of the word she'd faked at the table, which had made me feel older and unnecessary. Passing a resting security guard who was standing watch on a folding chair, my eldest child turned Alex Trebek.

"Dad, tell me again, who was the president who invented the folding chair?"

He wasn't horsing around—he didn't remember! I smiled broadly—they still needed me. Stop the clock, baby, I'm back!

24

Road Trip

What Happens in Dublin Stays in Dublin

t was like one of those cell phone service ads where a person asks a really important question and you don't hear the answer because the call gets dropped. But in this case I knew my dad was still there. I could hear him breathing. I don't know why he didn't answer me immediately; all I asked him was "Is there anyplace you'd like to visit before you die?"

Maybe I could have massaged it and asked, "anyplace you'd like to ever visit," so it did come out a little brusquely, but there was no putting the Ben-Gay back in the tube. He sat mute on his end of the line. Living apart since college, I really wanted to spend a week with him while I still could, which meant before I got too old and whiled away my days watching *The Price Is Right* while drooling into a bucket.

Come on, I thought, make up your mind. . . . Who are you, Anne Heche?

Eventually he replied, "I can't think of a place."

"Dad, I'll pay," I blurted out before my cheapskate gene had a second to kick in.

"Spend the money on your wife and kids. There's really no place I'd like to see."

I'd made my offer and he had declined. I would move on to other conversation, and I completely forgot my proposition until two days later, when he urgently phoned me at work. "I want to go to Ireland

and see where we came from." Growing up Irish, we knew our people came from county Cork or Killarney or something that started with a *c* or a *k* sound. The problem was that when our forebears arrived in this country, my grandma told me, they were too loaded to remember their previous street address.

"That's a great idea. I'll get on it today." That was husband code for "My wife will get on it today," and Kathy had us completely booked in two days.

"I know how much you hate to drive," she said, "so I got you guys a driver, in a stretch for a week."

A chauffeur and limo? I was positive I'd dialed my home number; why had Mrs. Donald Trump answered the phone? "Honey, we can't afford that."

"It's not a limousine," she said to her lone client. "It's a bus tour. This way the driver will tell you what famous rock you're looking at." Instantly I relaxed and removed my gold fillings from eBay.

A bus tour was perfect. That way we didn't have to worry about airport transfers or where to eat or stay while my father and I spent the week together talking about things fathers and sons need to talk about.

"Hey, Dad, pack your bags. I've got the tickets!"

"Swell, I just told my brother Phil about the trip."

Okay, that was good to hear, because that meant he really wanted to go. My dad and his brother shared the same values, history, and face. Phil was a little taller, a little broader, a bit pinker, but had the same Roman nose and twinkling eyes. A United States marine who proudly served in the Korean War, Phil returned home to Bancroft, Iowa, and started working at the town clothing store. It was the only job he ever had, and he loved it until the day he retired.

"I think your uncle Phil seemed a little jealous we were going to Ireland." This was exactly what children dream of: being able to treat their parents to something so spectacular that other family members will be envious and gossip about them at the next family reunion. Real life never lets you down!

"Uncle Phil's right. It'll be the trip of a lifetime," I said, beaming.

"Stephen, I didn't know what else to tell him. . . ."

"You are still going, aren't you?" There was urgency in my voice, prompted by a large cash purchase of nonrefundable tickets within the past hour.

"Absolutely, I'm going." He paused dramatically. "And so's your uncle Phil."

"Great . . . ," I said, in a voice that FBI analysts would say indicated I was not being completely truthful. But thanks to the Patriot Act, if speaking on an interstate telephone call, you're never obligated to tell the truth when talking to your parents.

"And, Stephen, one more thing . . ."

"Yes, Dad . . . ?"

"You're paying for your uncle's trip too."

The luck of the Irish had just run out. My once-in-a-lifetime father-son adventure to Ireland was in ruins; now I'd never have father-son heart-to-heart conversations in quaint neighborhood pubs while watching grown red-haired drunk guys dance in clogs. Wait a minute, I didn't like smoky pubs, and beer made me bloated, and I certainly never got the charm of the *Riverdance* phenomenon where shirtless men danced hard on wooden floors like they were from Terminex and their only weapon against termites was a pair of black patent leather dancing pumps.

I didn't want to pay for my uncle, and now the trip unexpectedly seemed like a monumental mistake. I could call my dad in a few days and say my boss wouldn't give me the time off. He'd never know. But then the little voice in my head reminded me that my father never asked me for anything, and it would mean a lot to him. Besides, my uncle Phil, a deacon in his parish, was one of the greatest sermonizers in Iowa history, and if I paid, with Phil's connections I'd surely wind up in the E-ZPass lane to eternal salvation.

Phil had always been there in my life. His wife, Jane, was my mom's best childhood friend and now they were my godparents, making sure I got a handsome seven-button dress shirt every year on my birthday until I turned twenty-one, which was apparently when the godparent statute of limitations ran out, forcing me to buy my own ready-to-wear.

"I'd be happy to pay for both of you," I said, and meant it, flat-out sounding like a dot-com billionaire who had bought Google at a dime a share.

Within a month my father and uncle and I were on a red-eye over the black Atlantic, flying from Newark to Shannon via Ireland's national airline, Aer Lingus, which loosely translated means "arrive intoxicated."

"Stephen, Phil," my dad pronounced as we wandered off the over-night flight into the blinding blaze of an Irish sunrise, "by this time next week, boys, we'll know where we came from."

"So let's get this party started!" my suddenly energized uncle Phil declared, which was jarring, as that quote was from a song by the Black Eyed Peas. I presumed Phil hadn't listened to Top 40 radio since Wolfman Jack went the way of the passenger pigeon, so maybe he was cutting loose because he was out of town with his brother and his nephew, Mr. Moneybags. Whatever got into Phil, I made a mental note to keep the deacon away from the tattoo and body-piercing castles.

"Top of the morning to you, gents," our driver and tour guide announced at the door of our gleaming fifty-passenger motor coach. With red but thinning hair, our driver would be considered height challenged; he was almost leprechaun sized, which made me feel bad when he struggled with our luggage, but to be fair, it was included in the price, and the physical lugging and loading surely saved him from paying for a gym membership.

"Ireland has forty shades of green," our Lucky Charms driver announced on the bus public address system as we pulled out of Shannon and headed for our week of fun. I think our guide, a terrific driver and wonderful storyteller, got hired because of his voice, an authentic combination of Pierce Brosnan and Bono. Whatever he said sounded like the official voice of Ireland, when in reality he was probably making up half of the stuff so we'd snap a photo, buy a T-shirt, or eat more boiled cabbage.

At a kilt-raising fifty-five kilometers an hour we spent our days circling Ireland's southern half. Aside from the Waterford crystal factory, where their slogan is "We make breakable stuff people can't afford," the only other place I'd ever heard of was the Blarney Castle, home of the Blarney Stone.

Legend has it that if you kiss the stone, you'll be blessed with the gift of gab, or "blarney." In reality, "blarney" was probably what tourists said when they discovered that to kiss the stone, you first had to pay seven euros (almost twelve dollars) for a Blarney Castle day pass, then climb slippery stairs to the highest part of the prehistoric ruin, where you'd lie on your back and inch out over the facade with the help of two strapping castle employees whose job was not to drop the customers, because five stories directly below the stone was a granite floor. This was not a tourist trap, it was a death trap. I was surprised an Irish personal injury attorney hadn't closed down this dump, where they'd been humiliating tourists since 1446.

"You gonna do it, Dad?"

"My back is killing me, Stephen. . . ."

"Uncle Phil?" Suddenly quiet and no longer our family's own hip-hop Reverend Run, he benched himself from the stunt. "Steve, the last time I was backward and upside down was in a Korean foxhole in '52."

Already out twenty-one euros (thirty-five bucks), I volunteered to be the first American-based member of my clan to canoodle the castle. As soon as the guy ahead of me kissed the stone, he was unceremoniously yanked back from the brink, and as he stood, he seemed momentarily dazed and dizzy. That was a new hazard I had not imagined—the possibility I would simply fall off the side. The Blarney boys waved me over, and as I approached, I instantly noticed they both had a whiff of lunch liquor on their breath.

"Okay, Jack and Daniel, let's go."

Surely puzzled by what the damned Yankee was talking about,

the handlers nonetheless pushed me out over the castle crevasse, allowing me to grab hold of two iron bars that framed the stone. At that moment I was upside down and flat on my back suffering from a bout of extra-dizzy vertigo. Trying to get it over as fast as possible, I gave it just a peck on her wall, scraping the end of my nose on the way back up.

"How did it taste?" the burly handler asked as he steadied me for the trip down.

"I've had better castle," I joked, dabbing the blood off the tip of my nose.

"Let me let you in on a little secret." He lowered his voice to explain that at night after the pubs closed, the local lads jumped the gate and came up there to pee on the stone that tourists would kiss nonstop the next day. Why he had selected me for this true confession was a mystery, but if he was trying to gross me out, he had picked the wrong guy. I'm a father of three who has no problem changing a poopy diaper with one hand while holding a Manwich in the other.

On the descent I started an hour-long hypochondriacal review of the possible diseases I could develop after positive lip contact with a Guinness-borne kidney infection. Once the bus pulled up at our hotel for the night we adjourned to the pub, where I had a double gin and tonic that was heavy on the gin, light on the tonic. Alcohol was a proven antiseptic. They always used booze in the westerns to cleanse a gunshot wound. It was the Irish equivalent of gargling with Purell.

In reality, I would have had the same drink anyway because going to a different pub each night was all we did. It was all anybody did—have you ever heard of anybody going to Ireland for the bowling? While Phil and I would sample the many chewy beers, my father would methodically research our family origins.

"You got a phone book?" he'd ask the bartender.

Dad wasn't looking for a specific phone number. He was looking for actual family members, people who spelled their names just like we did. He found a few families that were close, but they always messed it up with an extra letter or two. After five days, he'd checked the phone books in numerous restaurants, retail stores, and rail stations all over the Emerald Isle, and not once did he find our family name.

"Stephen, come here!" he called at the conclusion of a factory tour. At the pay phone over by the snack bar, he had found four families that spelled their names exactly like ours. Eureka! We had hard evidence of actual Irish relatives for the first time in our lives. A college researcher would certainly document such a momentous discovery by making a photocopy from the phone book, or at the very least making a detailed notation of the name, address, and phone number. My father had his own system: when he found a matching name, he'd rip that page out of the phone book and wad it up in his pocket.

Before we'd left America, I'd made an appointment at Ireland's National Library's Genealogical Service; that's where the world went to officially trace Irish heritage. "Gentlemen, please have a seat as I check the computer," the clerk said in a Brenda Fricker voice.

"Mr. Doocy, it looks as if your family first settled . . . oh." Midsentence she paused in a jarring way, as if a dire warning had just popped up on her screen from Interpol that we were armed and dangerous cat burglars from America, and she should quietly alert the proper authorities.

"What's the matter?"

"I can't say for sure, but it appears . . ." She dangled the secrets of our family history away from us a few seconds longer, until she revealed, "Your family's records . . . were destroyed in the fire. Sorry."

Fire?

Stunning was the only way to describe finding out that the national government of your motherland says you do not officially exist in its database and neither do any members of what you thought was your family. We sat there sobered, as if we'd discovered that whenever our kids needed batteries, they took the ones from the smoke detector over our bed.

"They called it the Four Courts fire. It was in 1922." She recounted how that blaze wiped out many Irish families' histories. I looked over at my father, who had a blank but pained expression, the same sad look as when everybody excuses himself from the table and stiffs you with an astronomical dinner bill.

"There's another possibility." The clerk threw us a lifeline. "Your name is misspelled."

"It's D-o-o-c-y," my dad said.

"I know that's how *you* spell it, but over the last one hundred fifty years, when many family names were entered into the county record books for births, baptisms, deaths, and land purchases, sometimes incorrect information was recorded."

That made perfect sense. Long before computers or microfiche or college-ruled paper, names and dates and fates were scrawled in big books by well-intentioned but illiterate Irish record keepers.

"Sometimes the handwriting in the book was hard to decipher, so the person recording it would have to make his best guess what it said. Sadly, many a name has changed through history because of bad penmanship." She stopped for a moment and then added an additional reason for poor spelling. "Then again, the writer may simply have been drunk."

Uncle Phil stated the obvious. "I vote for the drunk explanation."

"That means," the clerk continued, "your real family name could be Doocey, with an *e*, or Dewsy, or Dancy, or Dooley, or Deacy." Then she shocked us with one more bit of news. "If you see an Irish name and it starts with the letter *d*, there's a relatively good chance you're related."

And with that, I turned from a public scallywag of unknown heritage to a direct descendant of Phil Donahue. That was an explanation we would embrace—that our blood relatives had been misspelling our name since Saint Patrick drove the snakes that peed on the Blarney Stone off the island.

Relieved that our family did have some kind of roots, although misspelled ones, my father summoned the words to address this major development. "Maybe those kids in your school were right," he said, looking directly at me. "You might be a Doofus, after all!"

The people upstairs in the archive stacks probably wondered what prompted the bedlam in the basement. I cannot remember a time we laughed longer or louder. Our genealogical quest complete, we devoted the rest of the trip to just laughing it up. We didn't mingle much with the twenty other mostly Americans on the bus tour until we pulled over and posed for a class photo in a lush green meadow. I found myself standing next to a thirty-something woman I'd seen riding up front with a woman I presumed was her mother, and I asked her how she was enjoying the ride around the island.

"It's okay, but there's too much sitting and not enough shopping." She asked me if I missed the shopping.

"Are you kidding? I hate to shop. Luckily, my wife loves to. She calls it retail therapy."

"Your wife?"

"Fifteen years, three kids."

"Wow, we saw a forty-year-old guy traveling with his father and uncle, and we thought you were gay."

"Who thinks I'm gay?"

"Everybody on the bus . . . except probably your father and his brother."

"Actually, my dad considers me bi," I joked, "because on this trip, I have to buy everything."

She apologized for jumping to conclusions. "So why'd you leave your wife at home and take the Sunshine Boys for a ride?"

An excellent question from a total stranger. I explained that my mother had died just a few months earlier, and at that time my mom and dad had been planning the trip of a lifetime to Hawaii. After she passed away, even though he'd already bought the tickets for the trip, my dad refused to go without my mom.

"I just can't do it, Stephen," he'd told me, and that's why I asked him if there was anyplace *else* in the world that he'd like to go, and of course that's what got us those three spots on the bus.

"I've been away from home a long time," I told her. "I wanted to spend some time with my dad. My uncle was a bonus."

A bittersweet trip for my dad—I'm sure he'd have loved to share it with my mom.

I was also a bit bummed out because at the beginning of our adventure I'd thought we'd roll up to a charming pub on a cobblestone street in a town we'd never heard of, and there would be our family name above the door. We'd walk in and somebody would say, "We've been waiting for you. I'm your third cousin. Call me Angus."

For a change, I was in no hurry to go back, because I was appreciating my father for the first time not as my dad but as a man. He was funny and smart, and I couldn't believe the good fortune that I was related to him. After seven days and 220 bus miles, our trip was complete; the memories cast, it was time to go home. As our afternoon flight was starting to descend over Maine, I leaned over to my father, who was memorizing the Atlantic coast. I said, "That was fun, wasn't it?"

He paused for a moment. I'd clearly caught him deep in thought. "I felt like I was thirty all over again."

When he was thirty, I was only ten. Every Saturday morning my father the traveling salesman would holler up the stairs "You coming?" I'd roll out of bed and hop in his truck, not knowing where the day would take us. I was my father's sidekick.

At lunch we'd stop at a roadside café where we'd order whatever the cook was having himself, and then by midafternoon, after a dozen sales calls, we'd usually wind up at Reilly's gas station shooting the breeze while nursing Dr Peppers that always tasted best when they had half a bag of peanuts bobbing in the top. By suppertime we'd pull up at home, having spent the entire day talking and laughing about nothing in particular.

But as I look back now, I see that on those long rides with my dad I learned more about people and places and politics and how the world works than I ever would from anybody else. At the time it seemed like I was keeping him company, but it was much more than that. I was getting a master's degree in life from my pop. Back then, the reason I went was to spend time with my dad. It was exactly like our week on the bus.

My father was prophetic when he said that first day in Ireland, "By this time next week, we'll know where we came from."

We saw where *he and I* came from, a place long ago and far away, where the thirty-year-old father was accompanied everywhere by his son. It was now thirty years later and the young man was now sleeping in the corner of a nice hotel room on a roll-away as two snoring brothers and members of AARP enjoyed the four-hundred-thread-count Irish linen sheets. That weeklong stiff neck from the Hide-A-Bed cost me nine thousand dollars, which I'd gladly pay again to be their tagalong traveling companion.

Ireland had a big impact on us. The enduring legacy of our trip is that a day probably doesn't go by when in over a dozen establishments that we visited, somebody who's trying to phone Jimmy Donnelly, Mary Dancy, or Billy Dooley simply can't, thanks to my father.

"Where's the *d* page of your phone book?"

If he really wanted it, he could find it half a world away in my father's top dresser drawer, safely parked next to a couple of unused tickets to Hawaii.

25

Loose Ends

Goodnight Moon

Fatherhood is like Wikipedia, some parts based in fact, others just made up along the way. As a new dad I tried to plan ahead, but as I have learned over these many years, nothing ever works out exactly the way it was supposed to, so you have to ad-lib all the time. I have learned that the best plan is to be surprised.

My children were the reason I got up for decades in the middle of the night like a milkman to go to work. They are appreciative of the sacrifices my wife and I have made, and I hope they will make the same for their children. I am blessed to have been able to spend good times with these kids, but I know that in three years the last one will be off to college, and my perfect wife will be stuck with a creaky wheeze bag who rushes home from the Early Bird Special to watch Fred Barnes beat up Morton Kondracke and vice versa.

I'm already in bedtime-story withdrawal. Nobody wants me to read *Goodnight Moon* or *Love You Forever* to her anymore. The next domino to fall will be holding hands. The only regular hand-holder I've got left is Sally. On September 11, 2001, by ten o'clock in the morning, children at her school just outside New York were being called into the principal's office, and Sally was worried when some of them left screaming. Her third-grade teacher, who had gotten married on the top of the World Trade Center, was sitting on the floor crying; she told everybody that airplanes had hit skyscrapers in New York, the buildings had fallen, and many people were dead. Sally heard that and thought, My daddy works in a New York skyscraper. He must be dead.

She sat in her classroom for five hours thinking that she would never see me again. She was expecting bad news when she got home. My wife told her I was fine, but because the bridges and tunnels were closed to traffic, I was stuck on the island of Manhattan for two nights and three days. When I eventually got home, the tears were pouring down her cheeks when she ran to hug me. She had never been much of one to hold hands, but starting that day whenever we were together she'd reach out for her father's hand. Sally is now a high school sophomore, and to her credit she gladly grips and grins when we walk together or during the Lord's Prayer in church, but just like everything else, I know those hand-holding days are numbered.

This past weekend my wife, Kathy, drove my daughters and me down toward Washington, D.C. Three hours into the trip I noticed that my chauffeur wife was steadily watching her rearview mirror for what I presumed was a tailgater.

"Look at Mary," she whispered.

With her face pressed against the headrest, my college girl was asleep with the exact same face we'd see when she'd doze off in her car seat almost twenty years earlier. The exact same face.

Before we were blessed with these kids friends would say, "You better see plenty of movies before the baby comes along because after that, you'll be busy for a *long time*." They were right—we were busy. But that *long time*, between Huggies and beer pong, wasn't really that long. One year I was reading them books they could chew upon, the next showing how to tie a shoe, and then it was how to ride a bike in the driveway. Their homework got too hard for me to help, so I hired tutors when necessary, and in one final act of bravery I put stamps on their college applications.

Pooft!

They were gone.

It goes fast.

An ambitious little boy, I dreamed that one day I'd invent something or find a cure for a dreaded disease or write the great American novel that would be turned into a movie starring Meredith Baxter Birney, but somewhere along the way I discovered that those things were just lines on a résumé, and the older I got the more I realized that true immortality comes only from starting a family.

When I reminisce about my own childhood I see myself in the scratchy eight-millimeter home movies of the 1960s, chasing my sisters around the backyard after dinner drives to the Tastee-Freez, and on Friday nights we'd go to the Rocket Drive-in already wearing our pajamas because we'd fall asleep halfway through the second feature, unless it involved gunplay. In my head I'm twelve years old and my dad still has jet-black hair on the top, and I can still hear my pretty blond mom's laugh, which was so infectious that even if you were paralyzed with anger, you'd wind up snorting along with her. Now my mom is forever gone, and my only complete family reunion is when I close my eyes. I am lucky I have nice things to remember.

My college friend Carly Ellis told me that one of her greatest regrets was not saying "I love you" to her father at the end of a phone call, because the very next call she got was that her dad had been killed by a train while he was driving home. That was the day I stopped saying "Good-bye" to everybody, because you just never know. I substituted *See you later* because I never want that shared moment to be our last.

I hope my stories have reminded you of your own father or grandfather or maybe even mom or kid tales. I hope that your relationship with your family is good, but if it is not, something as simple as a letter or a phone call can be a terrific first step. Life is so much more complete when you go through it with people you share a bloodline with.

The key, I believe, is togetherness. At our house, dinner runs almost an hour from first bite to last laugh. Every one of the day's high crimes and misdemeanors is rehashed. Last week my wife told the table that she'd read there was a mini crime spree in our neighborhood, with an alarming number of random house robberies. Suitably

scared, we adjourned to watch a movie and promptly forgot about
the police blotter.

This afternoon my son, Peter, who was home on a break, was taking a nap when he heard somebody stirring on the front porch. No
car or truck in the front driveway. He peered out a side window and
spotted a powerfully built stranger staring through first the front
windows and then the front door.

The random house burglar, and he's casing the joint.

A regular viewer of *America's Most Wanted,* Peter knew that if that
man was about to rob us, he'd first ring the doorbell, and if nobody
came, he'd break the glass and help himself to our family's priceless
black velvet portraits.

Ding-dong.

If Peter did not answer the door, the burglar would find him
crouching behind the NordicTrack, and that never ends well. I have
told my children a million times not to open the door to total strangers, but Peter at age twenty was a man himself and made a strategic
choice that could change his life. On the way to the front door he
made a quick detour, and then, feeling his heartbeat in his throat, he
opened the door a crack.

"Hi, just checking to see if anybody was home," the guy said, just
like in the movies. Next stop chalk outline. "Can I come in?"

Wearing blue jeans and a ripped T-shirt, the guy insisted he was
there to fix our Internet. *Good cover story: where was his uniform or
Internet repair truck?* Just back home from college, Peter didn't know
whether our Internet was on the fritz, but he did know that if it was
not working and he turned the guy away, it could be a week before a
repairman, real or felonious, returned, and his father would miss important spam e-mail advertisements for herbal Viagra or announcements that he'd won the Scottish lottery.

Going against everything I had taught him, he invited the stranger
into our home.

"It's over there." Peter pointed the man toward the room with the
computer. A Greta Van Susteren devotee, he knew not to lead the

guy into the room or he'd get jumped from behind and pounded into something with the consistency of guava jelly.

The "repairman" stood next to the computer, completely befuddled by the tangle of wires under our iMac. Peter got a terrible feeling in his craw that the man knew nothing about computers and in a moment Peter would face the ultimate moment of truth.

"Do you have a flashlight?" the guy asked.

"Sorry," Peter said, knowing that a flashlight was the kind of blunt object these types were always using on dummies who opened front doors to local outlaws.

Peter stood there fully prepared for the worst. Unbeknownst to the interloper, just before he opened the door, Peter had gone into the kitchen, where he'd grabbed the deadliest thing in our house, a Smith and Wollensky steak knife, the same one I lopped off the end of my finger with. At that moment, with the perplexed perpetrator bent over less than a yard from my son, Peter was gripping the wooden handle of the knife inside the front pocket of his North Face coat. One wrong sudden move and my son was ready to plunge it into the guy's rib cage.

Then it happened!

The stranger fixed the Internet.

"Modem power cable burned out," he announced, and within thirty seconds he replaced it with a new one from his pocket.

Peter didn't know that that morning I'd begged the Internet service provider to send somebody over to fix it. The repair guy parked his truck at the back of our driveway so he wouldn't block our cars, and he arrived in a T-shirt and not his uniform because he got called directly from a softball game.

"Next time don't answer the door," I pleaded during another lecture on personal safety, just relieved Peter didn't know I kept our improvised explosive devices under the sink next to the Drano.

Now that I examine what he did, I'm relieved he didn't forget momentarily that the cutter was in his pocket and sit on it.

"Excuse me, Fixit Guy, could you drive me to the hospital? I just impaled myself on the knife I was going to stab you with. . . ."

Thank goodness, nothing bad happened, but I keep returning to the larger question: *What was he thinking* when he opened that door? I keep coming back to the same answer: Peter has been faithfully watching and studying me for twenty years, and upon further review, the steak knife thing was definitely something of which I was capable.

Monkey see, monkey do.

A chip off the old block.

Like father, like . . . you get the idea.

As I think about it, who needs Smith & Wesson when you've got Smith and Wollensky?

I read somewhere that sibling rivalry ends at age fifty, but parental worry has no expiration date. A dad's job is never done. Fatherhood is a lifetime sentence, much like what Peter could have gotten if he had used that steak knife on the Verizon guy.

26

The List

What Every Father Must Teach His Child

1. Never drink anything out of a boot.
2. Giggle at something every day. Just know laughter is not the best medicine; medicine is the best medicine.
3. Be prepared, if you must use a public toilet; squat, hover, and flush with your foot.
4. When at an unfamiliar restaurant, always order the menu item that is featured in a box. If no box, order what the waitress had.
5. Don't cry, but if you must, be brief.
6. Expect the unexpected. Who says Dustin Hoffman won't join the cast of *Hannah Montana*?
7. Tell the truth, unless somebody is asking if his pants make him look fat.
8. When in a bar fight go for the eyes, figuratively not literally.
9. A yellow light at an intersection means slow down, and proceed with caution, after you check the mirror for cops.
10. Watch your language; if you say, "Nice rack," you'd better be talking about the lamb.
11. When in doubt, call home.
12. Dad will always love you, even when a child asks why he has all those wrinkles and his breath smells like Jack cheese.
13. Hygiene is important, but only use the hand sanitizer discreetly

so the world doesn't know you're a germ freak on a par with Michael Jackson.

14. Shakespeare said, "Neither a borrower nor a lender be"; I say, "Don't rob a bank."

15. Don't live your life by a checklist. That's silly.

THANK-YOUS AND SHOUT-OUTS

This is a book about fathers, and I must start by acknowledging a man who has been like a father to me and many at the Fox News Channel, Roger Ailes, who is not only the most powerful man in television news, but in reality a great dad. He has been my mentor for fifteen years; I love this man as much as one guy can love another without getting an apartment in the Village.

Years before Roger would return my phone calls, Beth Ailes saw something and hired me. Beth once had me host a parenting show that helped make me a much better dad and eventually led to the book that you are holding. Without her right now you'd probably be holding *The O'Reilly Factor for Pets*. Thank you, Beth.

To my TV brothers and sisters, Brian Kilmeade, Gretchen Carlson, Alisyn Camerota, and Andrew Napolitano, thank you for making it easier to get up every day at 3:27 A.M. Behind the scenes at *Fox & Friends*, Lauren Petterson, Gresham Striegel, Jennifer Williams, Maral Usefi, and Jennifer Cunningham, thank you for whispering things in my ear; now I have seven voices in my head. That's normal, right?

To Bill Shine, Suzanne Scott, Joel Cheatwood, Woody Fraser, John Moody, Brian Lewis, Irena Briganti, Jack Abernethy, Dianne Brandi, Chris Silverstri, Cristina Cassese, Judy Laterza, and other Fox News big shots whom I have counted as friends in some cases for over two decades, thanks for everything. Please don't turn on me now.

To the *O'Reilly Factor* squad, Mr. Bill, David Tabacoff, Amy Sohnen, Rob Monaco, and of course my cross-desk rival, Martha MacCallum, just know when I miss a quiz question, I'm just trying to look human.

To the coffee-guzzling, bagel-munching men and women of Studio E who work the dawn patrol, you're marvelous; don't ever change a thing, except the lighting. Jeisohn and Maureen, remember, nobody needs to know that Hannity uses a Lady Remington shaver.

You would be holding a mess of mimeographed musings on three-ring-binder paper if not for the supportive team of yes men and women I have at the publisher William Morrow. When editor par excellence Mauro DiPreta (screen name ieditnaked) suggested I write a book on fatherhood, I trusted his judgment and started writing even though in my heart I wanted to write a book on Canada's professional women's volleyball league.

Thanks as well to the rest of my team at HarperCollins, Lynn Grady, Jennifer Schulkind, Pamela Spengler-Jaffee, Richard Aquan, and the very big cheeses, Michael Morrison, Lisa Gallagher, and Jane Friedman, who'll return my urgent pleading phone calls as soon as this album goes platinum.

To superagent Bob Barnett, who will read this single paragraph and bill me for a quarter hour, thank you for the advice not to sell the movie rights to Vivid Video.

Premiere Speakers Bureau helped coordinate my book tour and other promotional activities. Thanks to Duane Ward and his gang in Nashville for putting me in a rock star's tour bus! When I pulled up to a Books-A-Million location, some woman thought the Eagles were onboard and threw me her panties. They didn't fit so I threw them back.

Thank you to true friends who shared their ideas and stories: Peter and Blanche Johnson, Todd and Madeline Van Duren, Rodger and Beverly Rohde, Deb and Rodger Rohde Jr., Faith and Ray Van Duren, Jim and Mary Madormo, Greg Ciccone, Eileen and Bud Hansen, Judy and Mike Lee, Mary and Jack Vossler, J. R. and Laura Frank, Goldie Weisz and Sileshi Petro.

Thanks to my in-laws, Rob and Gwen Gerrity, Dub and Randa Gerrity, and Big Daddy Joe Gerrity.

The most sincere thanks go to my family, first and foremost my wife, Kathy, who is not only the best mother I have ever known and a loving, wonderful wife, but also one of the best partners a guy writing a fatherhood book could have, as she scribbled notes in the margins with verbatim quotes from the actual day these stories took place. You are a gem, and you're all mine.

And of course to the three miracles who are the reason I am a father, Peter, Mary, and Sally. Thank you for being not just good kids, but funny, wise, thoughtful, and downright inspiring people.

To my sisters, Cathy, Lisa, Ann, and Jenny, and their families; the miles may separate us, but not in my heart.

And finally to my father, Jim, the man I hope to be when I grow up. Thank you for showing me the way.

Steve Doocy
New York City
2008

P.S.: Allow me to extend a special word to all who bought this book, got the CD audio book, or checked it out at your local library. I told readers of my first book that as a journalism student it was a lifelong dream to write a book that somebody would read to the very end. Thanks to you, that dream just came true.